DATE LOANED

A

ART CENTER COLLEGE OF DESIGN LIBRARY
1700 LIDA STREET
PASADENA, CALIFORNIA 91103

DID BRITAIN MAKE IT ?

British design in context 1946–86

DID BRITAIN MAKE IT ?

British design in context 1946–86

Edited by Penny Sparke

The Design Council

Did Britain Make It?
British design in context 1946–86

Published in the United Kingdom by
The Design Council
28 Haymarket
London SW1Y 4SU

Typeset by Input Typesetting Ltd
London SW19 8DR

Printed by Chorley & Pickersgill

Designed by Mike McCarthy

British Library CIP Data

Did Britain make it? British design in
context 1946–86
    1. Design, Industrial—Great Britain
    —History—20th century
    I. Sparke, Penny II. Design Council
    670'.941   TS57
ISBN 0 85072 168 7

Contents

Introduction

The occasion, and excuse, for this book is the 40th anniversary of the 'Britain Can Make It' exhibition which was held at the Victoria and Albert Museum in London in 1946, just a year after the end of the Second World War. Forty years on seemed the right moment both to reassess the significance of that extraordinary event and to think about the changes that have taken place since then.

1986 is both similar to and dissimilar from 1946: today's mood of economic recession and high unemployment does, on the surface at least, have something in common with the Age of Austerity which affected the lives of everyone living on British soil in the decade following the War. In contrast, however, those days were characterised by a sense of unrelenting optimism and belief in the future which penetrated every area of public life, and which was certainly much in evidence at Britain Can Make It. Today this is less apparent and it is harder to discover a confident idea of the future within contemporary culture: the dominant styles of the day are nostalgic and revivalist. Our attitude to the future of manufacturing in this country is also predominantly pessimistic, at least where mass production is concerned, and our former overriding faith in technology is somewhat dulled in an age when it has given us the power to destroy ourselves.

Britain Can Make It was, without doubt, an enormously popular event. Deprived of new products (with the exceptions of Utility furniture and fashion) the British public had had to 'make do and mend' during the War years and it was, therefore, eager and ready to confront the rich feast of products that British manufacturers were, in theory at least, preparing for it in peacetime. Whether the public was delighted or dismayed by the goods it actually saw there, as an event, the exhibition had a tremendous impact on the people who queued for hours to get in to see it. That impact is hard now to reconstruct, or even to imagine. With the expansion of the consumer society from the late 1950s onwards has come a surplus of products available to a broader-than-ever section of the population: more people buy more consumer goods today, whether well or badly designed, than they did in 1946 and, as a result, the 'shock of the new' is harder to achieve.

The concept of design itself has also changed radically. In 1946 design simply meant that a product had been thought out visually and technically, and that it should, as a result of this, improve the quality of the life of the individual who owned and used it. Today design has become a much more public and publicised concept, associated not

1

simply with function and with 'good taste' but increasingly with social status—hence the insertion of the word 'design' into the everyday environment and the addition of the word 'designer' to sell a range of goods from jeans to scissors. It would be difficult, if not impossible, today to mount a design exhibition with the same, simple didactic intentions that the Council of Industrial Design had in 1946: it would have to be a much more complicated exercise, and probably wouldn't work. For that reason alone it is worth looking back at Britain Can Make It and trying to understand what was meant by the word 'design' in 1946, how it affected the people who came into contact with it, and how it has evolved and changed in the intervening years.

In order to try to make some sense of what amounts to a history of British design since the Second World War, this book is divided into six parts, each of which focuses on a theme which is directly related to the history of design in this period. All the themes emerge from Britain Can Make It itself which set out to consider design in the context of everyday life. Thus it is impossible to discuss design in this sense without considering its impact on the public; its relationship with manufacturing industry; the way in which it is affected by changes in the structure of retailing; the evolution of the designer as a practising professional; and the efforts of design promotion and reform bodies to influence mass taste. What is omitted by the decision to focus on these particular themes is a discussion, in this period, of style for style's sake—a subject covered in detail elsewhere — and an account of the design theory of the period, which may or may not have had an influence on design practice. This was considered to be too far removed from the realm of everyday life which is central to this book.

In keeping with the spirit of Britain Can Make It the basic questions that underpin all the material and discussions in this book are 'How has design influenced everyday life?' and 'What role has it played in influencing the way that Britain has evolved since the war, economically, socially and culturally?' Britain Can Make It projected a bright image of the future in which the newly formed professional industrial designer and the presence of design in all the manufactured products selected for it, were seen to be important. Their role was both to establish Britain as a manufacturing force to be reckoned with on the world market and to raise the level of public taste and thereby the quality of everyday life in Britain. This book sets out to discover whether or not this particular dream ever came true.

The first chapter examines exhibition design itself and establishes Britain's international importance in that sphere. It is an area which has been much neglected and badly needs reassessing. Britain Can Make It was James Gardner's first major project as an exhibition designer and 1986 provides the perfect opportunity to look back both at 1946 and at Gardner's career. It is Gardner, more than anybody else, who went on to turn his personal style of exhibition designing into an international phenomenon. Giles Velarde's interview with Gardner emphasises the originality of the Britain Can Make It display which, in certain ways, outshone the products exhibited. One contemporary critic described the exhibition as 'a glittering frame for a mediocre picture'.

Part 2 moves into a discussion of the policies and ideology that underpinned the Council of Industrial Design's campaign, from 1946 onwards, to reform standards of design in this country. Design promotion has played an important role through this period by providing the measuring stick against which most judgements about 'good design' have been made. Britain is one of the few countries to have a state-funded design promotion body and its work, from the 1946 exhibition right up to the present day, has been central to most of the major discussions about design that have taken place. This book prefers, however, to analyse the Design Council's achievement critically rather than simply to 'pat it on the back' as so many other accounts have done. Jonathan Woodham undertakes such an analysis in the context first of Britain Can Make It and then through an interview with Lord Reilly, a former director of the CoID, to hear 'from the horse's mouth' how the Council defined its role in the 1950s and 60s.

From here the discussion moves on to yet another theme which was highlighted at Britain Can Make It and which has been an important element in the evolution of British design since then: the emergence of the professional consultant designer. In order to examine the range of the professional designer's activities in this period, Part 3 focuses on two very different designers, the first of whom is a graphic artist whose experience during the Second World War made him a unique figure. The second chapter, written by Wally Olins, a director of a consultant design office, deals with the evolution in Britain of the American-inspired consultant design team involved with a wide range of briefs, from corporate identity to product design. Abram Games and Wally Olins are not only at two different ends of the design spectrum, their experiences, taken together, also span the period since 1946.

Part 4 moves out from the exclusive territory of design into the 'real world' and confronts the gritty question of how British manufacturing industry has used design and the designer in the years since 1946. Once again two contrasting areas have been selected to suggest the range of possibilities — the first a traditional, craft-based industry, namely textiles, and the second a newer, technologically orientated industry, namely consumer electrical and electronics. The aim of this section is not to criticise the attempts of British industry to integrate design into its activity but rather to examine the special circumstances that have made British mass manufacturing evolve in the way that it has, and to explain exactly why design, except in an exclusive sector, has never had the high profile that it has in a country like Italy. This is not merely an excuse to 'have another go' at British industry but rather an opportunity to examine possible ways forward for it in the light of the lessons of its immediate past. (This is the longest chapter in the book as it is the one which presents the greatest problems.)

From manufacturing the discussion moves directly into the logically related area of retailing, and Part 5 shows how the relationship of retailing with design and taste has been of vital importance in the period since 1946. A fascinating story emerges, revealing one of the means through which public taste is shaped; it shows how, in the 1940s and 50s, different retailing structures affected design in different ways. The two examples of fashion and furniture have been selected as retail case studies because the first represents a highly expendable product and the second a much more durable one, with different consumer implications. The parallels that emerge between the two accounts emphasise the strength of influence of retailing modes themselves.

The question of retailing leads directly into the heart of the discussion about the way British consumers have changed since 1946 in their response to the designed environment. Part 6 looks at the vexed question of public taste and its sociological significance, a subject which is too vast and complex to treat in any depth in this short section. The essays by Lucy Bullivant and Catherine McDermott — both historians of modern design — home in on the gap that existed, both in the 1940s and 50s, between the ideology of design promotion and the values of the public at large. It is an area that raises important issues about the success or otherwise of design promotion.

Together, these themes converge on the role of design within post-War British economics, society and culture; collectively they address an analysis of design in action and raise a number of fundamental issues about the strengths and weaknesses of British progress in this period. This book does not, in the end, seek to make judgements but rather to direct questions away from the somewhat clichéd assumptions that usually dominate discussions of this sort. It isn't enough simply to state, for instance, that 'the British public has no taste', that 'the British manufacturer refuses to employ designers', that 'all the best British designers go and work abroad', or even that 'design is the answer to all Britain's problems'. It is the reasons behind these assumptions that are interesting, not the assumptions themselves, whether true or false. By describing things as they *have* happened rather than as they *should* have happened, there is a chance that some reasons, and by implication some solutions, might arise in the process.

The strongest similarity between 1946 and 1986 is the shared belief in design's powers of salvation to bring the country from a position of economic weakness to one of economic strength. What 1946 was also committed to—perhaps more so than today—is the idea that 'good design' should improve the quality of the everyday life of the ordinary man and woman, not only (as we tend to discuss design in social terms today) those of the disabled, the elderly and the inhabitants of the

Third World. Britain Can Make It was about the quality of life in post-War Britain, a quality which, in 1946, combined traditional values with those of the modern world. It is, I feel, the overriding lesson that 1946 has to teach us and the one which we would do well to reinject into discussions of design in 1986, although now with a little less sociological naivety.

Part 1

Exhibition Design

Giles Velarde is an exhibition designer at the Geological Museum in London. James Gardner was the chief designer of the Britain Can Make It exhibition and has worked as an exhibition designer since then both in Great Britain and abroad. In this first chapter Velarde interviews Gardner — with whom he has co-operated over the years on a number of exhibition projects — and finds out both what it felt like to work on the 1946 exhibition and what Gardner has been doing since then. The ensuing discussion provides an overview of the main achievements in British exhibition design since the war and establishes Gardner as one of the most important exponents of his art during that period, as well as showing how his influence has been felt internationally.

James Gardner's 'Story of the Earth'
exhibition in the Geological Museum,
designed in 1972

GILES VELARDE INTERVIEWS JAMES GARDNER

James Gardner built his first exhibition for Shell before the Second World War. Today he is probably the best known exhibition designer in the world. Over the past half-century he has moved from the commercial enterprises of his youth to museum exhibitions and galleries all over the world. I first knew of him during my early days as an exhibition designer. He was the godlike figure to whom all referred and deferred. He was, and still is, a brilliant innovator.

I first met Gardner when I started work at the Geological Museum. He had designed the immensely successful 'Story of the Earth' exhibition and I had been employed to set up a design department which was eventually to take over all exhibition work. We had to meet because the design of the next Museum gallery had been promised to him. I, of course, wanted to take it over. This was not possible but an extremely friendly agreement was arrived at, wherein Gardner designed the exhibition's thematic form and structure, thus controlling its general appearance, while I and my team designed the detail — largely the graphics and specimen displays. There was no argument and no discord, difficult though it must have been for him and his team. The end product, 'Britain before Man', is something of which neither of us is ashamed.

Introduction to the 'Electron' exhibition at the Geological Museum

9

Gardner is 'G' to all who know him. He has that artist's trick of referring to himself as G, and that is what I will call him from now on. G lives a long way up Hampstead's Haverstock Hill, past the giant and crumbling mansions and next to a friendly pub (a considered choice?) There he has built every designer's dream: his own studio and home. I don't think he ever stops designing or thinking about design; and to live surrounded by future schemes, present work and past successes suits him perfectly. We talked in his own room which was large, comfortable and peppered with mementos, models and ideas.

I asked him first if there had been a great deal of design consciousness about in 1946. Did people think in terms of design? Did they talk about designers?

'Only designers talked about design,' he claimed.

'But did the man in the street?' I asked. He thought not. G went on to explain that the War of course created a large gap for everybody. Before then our influences came from Europe: there had been the Surrealist exhibition, an exhibition on modern design in Germany, the Paris Exhibition in 1937, and some in Stockholm and Zurich in 1939. He didn't know who had designed the Surrealist exhibition, but recalled that it had been held in the Bristol Gallery, opposite where the Museum of Mankind now is. Images of it had stayed in the mind. Only people like Misha Black and Ashley Havinden knew about good design; the rest were ignorant of it. Art schools like the Slade were still preaching the 'old painting' in oils, full of picturesque peasant costumes and romantic rapture. The whole reason for Britain Can Make It after the War was to make people more aware about design.

I told him that I had read an article in a magazine of the period which referred to artists and industrialists getting together to produce better products. In this day and age, when the word 'design' is so much used, we would no longer dream of using the word 'artist' in that context, would we? G explained that in those days design was not really a profession; the idea hadn't really got off the ground. Designers were the poor students from art schools who had worked in factories and were bullied by the bosses, and the only magazines around which showed nice cosy interiors were ones like *Good Housekeeping*; the idea that the general public would be interested in that stuff was however laughable. The pre-War design world comprised a few architects and a few rather advanced agency and commercial designers — G put himself in this latter category.

We turned to Britain Can Make It. It seemed to me that there had been a strong theme on the lines of 'we developed this as a Spitfire and now we can use it as a saucepan'. I asked him what he had been thinking then. He replied that he had been briefed by Sir Stafford Cripps, who had collected the exhibits together with the Council of Industrial Design. Cripps maintained that they had got to get Britain into the design world in order to sell our products overseas (he was an intellectual — he understood this, said G). People needed cheering up, too. They hadn't seen anything for five years and still couldn't buy anything in the shops but plain china and Utility furniture — which was very well designed by Gordon Russell with some Swedish influence, but stark. Straight after the War we reverted to where we had been ten years before, to the good old Maples type of furniture, and Cripps was determined to change the status quo. He said we should display prototypes, and decided to get firms to make some so that, even if they didn't end up being manufactured, public excitement would be engendered. G was commissioned to package this exhibition, and so he 'did a lot of decor — it was all Barnum and Bailey', but it succeeded, he felt, and made him the name for being a rather airy-fairy designer. He hastened to say that the idea was not to encourage the British to buy goods so much as to encourage manufacturers to produce well designed goods for overseas selling. The problem was how to design a show that would look complete in every detail, even if they did not get any exhibits.

He concocted a new plan in which the goods were not presented directly to the eye, as they might have been in a shop, but tucked round corners, behind screens and in little alcoves so the visitor was attracted by the decor and the mystery. It introduced a surprise element and kept the visitor's attention on one group of exhibits at a time and proved most successful. G claimed that Cripps had great vision; we had not had a Member of Parliament in power like him before or since, for he was not only concerned to give the British public a boost, but also to regain our place in the export world.

I asked whether he had found well designed things for the exhibition. Some, he said; but there might be two kettles on display: one a prototype and the other just in production. There was a radio set designed by Minns which never actually went into production and a section with products designed for the future. Henrion designed a sewing machine that was never made. Coates did a space ship and had a baby's pram with a radio built into it. These things were really more concepts of what might be produced than actual products.

There was one section on design itself, devised by Misha Black of the recently established Design Research Unit. G elaborated: during the War the then Ministry of Information (now the COI) had employed a group — mainly 'flat' artists — to produce propaganda: 'Dig For Victory' and 'Join the WVS' were among their most memorable achievements. The group included Misha, Jimmy Holland and Milner Gray. When the War ended the Stewarts Agency backed them financially to start DRU, and so Misha was at that time 'employed' by Stewarts. All the objects in this section had come in from the manufacturers; the Council of Industrial Design collected them all together and chose the best to exhibit. G had been called in to decide how many objects could be displayed in the space available.

I asked G whether, looking back to those days, he thought people were naive about design. He replied that in one way we were all naive, because then we actually thought there was a thing called progress; we believed that design was always improving; that, at that moment, we were as good as we had ever been, and that in the future designers were going to be better, and architects too. We thought that until recently. In other words, we thought we were on a developing scale of improving design; it had not yet fallen into the business of international competition dictating styles. National designs and styles existed then, but now of course it has become competitive because glossy magazines have made it so. Forty years ago we really thought that the shapes we were making were better than anything that had been done before, and that we were in the process of perfecting something.

Was he talking about taste or function? He replied that the period during the War had encouraged designers to apply function to taste. The idea of function in design predominated in the minds of the few who were doing advanced design and architecture; for the general public it didn't exist. I asked him who were the giants of his youth, in the fields we were discussing. He thought for a long time, and confessed to being terrible at remembering names; but Wells Coates came to mind. The idea of function in design had been engendered by the Bahaus, the Swedes and the Central Europeans, but the first people to put it into general practice were the Americans; our post-War ideas about styling were very much influenced by their mass production methods.

I told him that when one thinks of exhibition and museum design over the past 40 years, it is G's name that is paramount for my generation of designers. Did exhibition designers exist when he was a young man? Were there people he wanted to emulate? He felt that this particular discipline hadn't really existed before the War. The first exhibition designers were sponsored in the 1930s by companies like Shell and ICI who brought people over from the continent, or by Frank Pick at London Transport. They were real entrepreneurs. He thought the best exhibition designs of that period were being done by the Swiss and the Germans — they were very austere and simple. Straight after the War G was fresh and ready to go, having done one exhibition which was for Shell.

Some of the earliest exhibits he did were completely uneducated, however: 'just ingenious bits of doo-dah', he calls them, 'with no tradition to back them up'. (One of the problems he has in being interviewed is that he describes himself as a 'self-made cooker-upper of things'; in other words, he feels that he is bad at intellectualising and has little confidence in his ability to articulate his ideas verbally.)

Did he think Britain *had* made it, since 1946? He was pretty sure that things would have been worse if there had not been a Britain Can Make It exhibition, but he didn't think that it had had the impact it should have done at the time. It died out very quickly. 'In Britain you can't just do it in one show — conservatism is too dug in'.

When the Festival of Britain came along in 1951, was he, I asked him, simply redoing the same thing? Was he still hammering at the same door? Yes, he replied, they were essentially the same group of exhibition designers but this time there were more of them, about ten in total. All of them had had commercial jobs by then, doing exhibitions and they were still very much influenced by post-War Europe and America. They were competing with exhibitions at Leipzig, Hanover, and with the Milan Triennales. Among them were Arthur Braven, Leslie Gooday, Ron Dickens, Hulme Chadwick and Basil Spence whom G brought in to 'architect' Britain Can Make It ('He muscled into ICI — a bit of a pusher.'). British Overseas Fairs Ltd had been a powerful

Gardner's display for the British Pavilion in Montreal, Expo 1966, showing elements of British pop culture of the sixties

dispenser of jobs, and G remembered what marvellous shows they had produced, great stands two or three floors high and great pieces of artwork. The client was not aware that the group was trying to compete in design excellence with the overseas designers from Switzerland and Czechoslovakia. The sad thing was that nobody was really backing them; the happy thing was that they were competing at that time very successfully. G endorsed my memory that British exhibition design in the 50s and 60s was right at the top in its field. Our contractors were too, he added, but they were killed by the trade unions.

1958 saw the opening of the Brussels World Fair. 'Who had masterminded the British exhibit there?' I asked. 'It was a bit of a joke,' he replied, adding that Cecil Cook, then Head of COI, had masterminded the South Bank Festival of Britain but had had a lot of trouble with inexperienced designers: Hugh Casson had done one part of it with G, Misha Black and Jimmy Holland had done the other, and G had also been given Battersea Park as well. Cecil Cook then got the job for Brussels, and by then he was completely fed up with designers as a breed. He must have thought G the most practical and easy-going, for, as G himself recalls, 'Do you know what he did? This will never happen again in the history of the world — he gave me the whole job of the British Pavilion to do'. G had to write the theme, appoint an architect, brief him on the building, provide all the exhibits and cost it. They did the whole enterprise as a package deal. G employed a researcher, and then got hold of Jacob Bronowski and others to advise him, so that he had a few names behind him. He then formed a committee which included Malcolm Sargent and John Cockcroft. Since these people knew nothing about design, they agreed to everything, and G therefore had a completely free hand.

He devised a show in which the ambiance and the detailed display gave importance to the exhibits: a great hall with banners and a portrait of the Queen, and shafts of coloured light. It was almost cathedral-like, in which tableaux of the famous were the saints. An art gallery was contrived where the frames contained working models of scientific developments instead of paintings. He had not been given sufficient money, however, and he turned half the site into a garden; but instead of remarking, 'the British can't afford a roof', people thought it a highly original solution. G had the Royal College of Art under Hugh Casson to work with him on that section, but he did all the rest of it himself.

G himself then raised a point about the Council of Industrial Design. He had got to know Sir Gordon Russell very well, and once said to him that he thought that Habitat had had far more influence on standards of design in Britain that the CoID. Gordon Russell told him, shortly before he died, that the attitudes in industry in Britain to designers were no better than they had been at the end of the War, even after all the effort and money put into the CoID.

I remarked that the Design Council were obviously interested in the display of good design, and in practically everything that we had spoken about so far the good design had been brought in by the designers involved or directed only towards selling overseas. 'Was there anything happening between 1958 and 1966?' I continued. G replied that during this period firms like Liberty's and Selfridges had had designers brought from Sweden to tell them how to display their goods. Woollands had had a marvellous team, as had Harrods. A window display right round the corner of Swan and Edgar was done by a man from Czechoslovakia. 'Can you imagine any shop in London doing that now?' G asked. 'It was a show; people came especially to look at the windows in crowds, as they do now in Saks in New York.'

'Do you think that The Design Centre as a permanent display of British goods has been of any real value over the past 40 years?' I asked him. After a long pause, G replied that actually, he remembered saying to Gordon Russell some time back, 'Why don't you get a big store, on a corner in Oxford Street, and make a big public show of well produced exhibits?' Russell had said, 'G, it's as much as we can do to find enough well designed objects to put in the little place we've got at the moment.'

'Well, what about the Design Council? Do you think that has had an effect?' I asked. He didn't. 'You see,' he said, 'the trouble with Britain is that we've got a built-in national characteristic of conservatism that goes right back to the landed gentry.' The only innovations there have been were the efforts of a few designers and entrepreneurs who had been overseas and brought foreign ideas back with them. He didn't think there was much indigenous British understanding of design at all. For him, introducing the concept was like the near-impossible task of trying to convert people from one religion to another.

I turned the conversation to Montreal in 1966. The two most exciting things that I remember being told about there were the Czech Pavilion and the British Pavilion. 'Yes,' he replied, 'the Czech Pavilion was super with a multiple slide show. The toy section had a tree that grew, then turned into plain wooden blocks, then into the toys on the branches. They had a gallery like a cave, hung with thousands of earrings and pendants, like stalactites. The British can't invent like that,' G said; 'that was Central European flair, but we catch hold of the ideas and use them.' I remembered that he had worked on the British Pavilion with Shaughan Kenny. 'Yes,' said G, 'he did an entrance section which was about the history of Britain; one went round on a revolve and saw groups of animated figures.'

G was busy on Evoluon, Philips' permanent exhibition in Eindhoven, when the COI asked him if he would do 'Britain Today', the great big centre section of the Pavilion at Montreal. Britain was in a pretty bad way financially and no theme had been devised for this centre section. Eventually, a theme was sent to him, written by a don in Oxford. It was so bad that G resigned and sent it back. The Head of the COI Exhibitions Division gave up a holiday to come and persuade him to change his mind. He did, but only on condition that he was to have a completely free hand, including the writing of his own script. After all, it had worked for Brussels.

'What did Kenny do, then?' I asked. G replied, 'Two things, and with real flair — he was a showman. He did the Funfair section, and the History section with a great revolve, starting with Alfred the Great, through Henry VIII to the present day. It had stunning lighting and sound effects, very modern for those days.'

Montreal was about the national character, rather than product design. The Pavilion did include some Carnaby Street clothes, and a mini car painted like a Union Jack — emblems of swinging London — but G felt that he wanted to be a little different and show what British people were really like. The first thing the public saw when coming down a long escalator was an archetypal British family: an old chap with his eldest son, who was a stockbroker; his wife with a feather boa; and the younger children a bit apart and more modern. (There were distinct reverberations of 1946 here.) To the visitors the family seemed typically British, so pleased with themselves were they. But the moving sign beside them read: 'The British — are they stuffed shirts? Hypocrites? Stiff-upper-lipped?' G remembers taking the Russian delegation round, and they didn't get it at all!

Gardner's archetypal British family at the 1966 Montreal Expo

I reminded G that he had designed some products, too — the area above the waterline of the QE2; and a riverboat. 'Were there others?' I asked. He said he had had a go in the early days: a ship's log, an oven for English Electric, and other odd things like a room heater, but that he did it no longer because the manufacturers now dictate to the designer, and want to re-use various bits and pieces, and vacillate. 'I like a quick answer, you know.'

I told him that the first thing I had ever seen of his that I had really appreciated properly was the Pilkington Glass Museum. It is a permanent exhibition of products and methods. G told me about other work he had done for the CoID, including a travelling exhibition which went all around Britain. 'Enterprise Scotland' was similar in character and took place 18 months after Britain Can Make It, in Edinburgh. The travelling exhibition must have been three or four years later, with the exhibits folded up in containers.

I suggested that we, as exhibition designers, tended to think of the necessary shape of a display, and then find a way of making it. I remembered Arthur Braven telling me that the sky-hook existed in exhibitions and that you can hang impossible ceilings and effects from the roofs of exhibition halls, but that architects need structure and support to build up everything from the ground. G in turn remembered that in the Independent Broadcasting Authority Gallery (a permanent exhibition in Knightsbridge), an architect who was a great friend went around with him and said, 'but you've got different heights everywhere — why don't you make them all level?' 'Most architecural constructions were so modular, orderly and boring,' he said.

'Do you agree,' I continued by asking, 'that, when talking to students, there was a real danger of killing something in the analysing? I find the exciting thing about the field we are in is that it often depends on the quirkiest of ideas.' He agreed enthusiastically. 'Formalising things destroys something,' he added. This reminded him again of the Britain Can Make It exhibition. 'The tradition was,' he said, 'to have a gallery with a walk-way, a feature at the end and displays at the side. There it all was, like a high street, all architected and Germanic. In 1946 we had done the reverse thing, partly because of Cripps' anxiety to have an exhibition, even if there were no exhibits. When the visitor came into the hall, he couldn't see any of the goods; he went round corners, in and out, and it made it more exciting.' G has always done that since. He takes people behind and round things. The same was happening in typography at that time; when G started, everything was centred on a page, 'Then,' as he describes it, 'suddenly one got a bit over there and a bit over here, and so on.'

'Britain Can Make It had a very convoluted plan,' I ventured. 'It was a very convoluted building,' he retorted. 'What were the crowds like?' I asked. 'Solid,' he replied. 'they hadn't seen anything for years!' 'How was it that people should be so interested, and that it should have had no real effect? Were they looking at it like a peep-show?' I asked. 'Yes,' he replied, 'and of course the stuff wasn't available in the shops for five years, so the effect wore off.'

I asked G what he would do to try and educate people about design. How did he feel he could lift people up from the morass of grisly ideas like having 15 different wallpapers in the same room? He thinks that the British attitude to life is still embedded in the 19th century, and that the only way to change thinking is to change the teaching in schools. 'Art schools?' I asked. 'No,' he replied, 'schools at basic level.' However he maintained the problem lay with the teachers. He did once

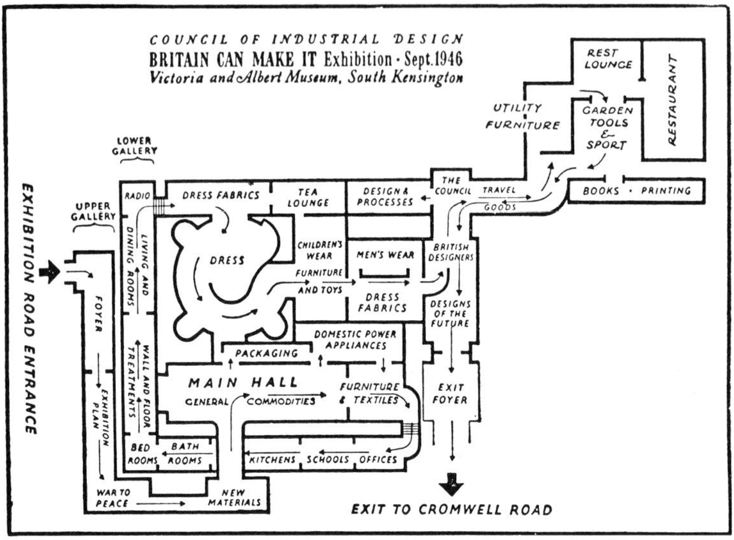
COUNCIL OF INDUSTRIAL DESIGN
BRITAIN CAN MAKE IT Exhibition · Sept.1946
Victoria and Albert Museum, South Kensington
REST LOUNGE
RESTAURANT
UTILITY FURNITURE
GARDEN TOOLS & SPORT
LOWER GALLERY
UPPER GALLERY
EXHIBITION ROAD ENTRANCE
RADIO
DRESS FABRICS
TEA LOUNGE
DESIGN & PROCESSES
THE COUNCIL
TRAVEL
GOODS
BOOKS · PRINTING
LIVING AND DINING ROOMS
DRESS
CHILDREN'S WEAR
MEN'S WEAR
BRITISH DESIGNERS
FURNITURE AND TOYS
DRESS FABRICS
DESIGNS OF THE FUTURE
FOYER
DOMESTIC POWER APPLIANCES
PACKAGING
WALL AND FLOOR TREATMENTS
MAIN HALL
GENERAL COMMODITIES
FURNITURE & TEXTILES
EXIT FOYER
EXHIBITION PLAN
BED ROOMS
BATH ROOMS
KITCHENS
SCHOOLS
OFFICES
WAR TO PEACE
NEW MATERIALS
EXIT TO CROMWELL ROAD

The plan for the Britain Can Make I exhibition designed by James Gardner and Basil Spence

persuade the Art master at Rugby to agree to take the pupils out of the school and down the high street. When they got back, they had to redesign five items he had selected, among them a lamp-post. As these boys were the businessmen of the future this exercise would, he felt, make them think about design. 'That,' said G, 'was what they ought to be doing in schools.' The upper middle classes were now design educated, but they were separate from the rest — that was, he suspected, probably the Habitat influence.

G went to Italy to do an exhibit for the Atomic Energy Authority in the 60s, and he decided that they wouldn't take any furniture with them. It would be easier to buy good contemporary things when they got there. So he arrived in Milan and asked for some very modern furniture. He was told there were two shops in Milan. One was closed, and the other had the lovely things one sees in *Domus*. He went in and ordered 'six of those chairs, one of those tables and four of those.' The reply was, 'delivery in three months'. They were samples, made up especially for wealthy people because there wasn't any market for them in Italy, either. The normal furniture shops were full of 'Tottenham Court Road, only worse'. I told him how similar it was in Stockholm in 1965, where everything in the shops was just as I had imagined it would be; but then I went to visit friends in the heart of Sweden, and their furniture and china was far worse than in Britain. This throws into question the usual clichés about the superiority of Italian and Scandinavian public attitudes.

'The difference,' said G, 'is that in those countries the intellectuals have to know about design in order to be generally cultivated. In Britain it is the reverse; only designers know about design. Intellectuals in Britain are not interested in visual things. We are literary, like the

Jewish people (G has just finished a big job in Israel). In Italy you can publish a magazine on engineering and have five pages of art in it; you can't do that here.' 'But,' I argued, 'in the 19th century there were some stunning natural designer–craftsmen, like Brunel and Telford.' He agreed readily, adding that *they* rose from the shop floor, and commented on the fact that Stephenson was the tenth son of a poor family in a slum. Arkwright came up from the floor of the mill. 'And did you know,' he said, 'that there was a little pavilion like the Crystal Palace in the Festival of Britain?' G added that he had found an old catalogue from an iron foundry in the Midlands, got in touch with them and discovered that they *still* had the original moulds. They cast some Victorian railings for him very cheaply.

G has had an enormous impact on design, especially museum and exhibition design, in the years between 1946 and the present day. In spite of this I think G would be happier to be remembered among that band of vastly creative, self-made Englishmen of the 19th century. His influence however *is* essentially 20th century. He practically invented the thematic exhibition in which theatrical models and devices are used to illustrate a story. G is the master of the visual metaphor, the simple comparison that helps the man in the street to understand often complex scientific or historic developments. Having worked all over the world, his influence is worldwide, often naively copied by designers who like his style but are unable to understand his methods. Every science centre built since 1966 has been influenced by Evoluon. Everyone who is about to embark on large-scale museum development either uses G, visits him or visits exhibitions he has designed. I have seen poor copies of parts of the 'Story of the Earth' all over North America.

G is completely at home with illusion, with animated displays and Pepper's ghosts. He is a conjuror, waving his wand over facts to make them as magic as fiction.

Part 2

Design Promotion

This part focuses on the role of, and the policies pursued by, Britain's major design promotion body — the Council of Industrial Design (later the Design Council) — in the period since 1946. Jonathan Woodham, a writer and historian of modern design who teaches at Brighton Polytechnic, takes an analytical look at the specific ideology that motivated the Council's work at the Britain Can Make It exhibition, providing at the same time an introduction to its major themes and contents. He describes, also, how these early policies evolved in the 1950s with, among other events, the opening of The Design Centre in 1956. In the second half of the chapter, Woodham interviews Lord Reilly, director of the Council of Industrial Design through the 1960s and early 1970s, establishing the way in which it interpreted its role during that time and asking whether or not it has, in Reilly's opinion, fulfilled the brief that it was set by the Board of Trade back in 1944.

The library at The Council of Industrial Design in the 1940s at Petty France

DESIGN PROMOTION 1946 AND AFTER
Jonathan M Woodham

As the Second World War was drawing to an end, attention was focused on the need to ensure Britain's future competitiveness in world markets. In a memorandum to the Board of Trade in 1944, the Industrial Art Committee of the Federation of British Industries (FBI) proposed the establishment of a Central Design Council to help bring this about.

On 19 December 1944 Hugh Dalton, President of the Board of Trade, announced the appointment of a Council of Industrial Design (CoID) in order to promote a better understanding of the importance of design in British industry; also to play 'a vital part after the War in stimulating the sale, at home and overseas, of a wide range of goods of which we can all be justly proud.' The magnitude of the task facing the new body was clearly outlined in Dalton's speech made at the inaugural meeting of the CoID on 12 January 1945:

> Something like an industrial revolution has taken place in the United States — a revolution of industrial design. It has made many of our exports old fashioned and less acceptable. It is not by accident but by prevision and provision, that there — and in Sweden, Czechoslovakia and Germany before the War — the design of machine-made goods has achieved a wholly new importance. . . . Our manufactured exports alone before the War totalled about £400 million, at least half of which was contributed by industries whose sales are bound to be greatly affected by design. And as we all know, after the War we must have at least 50% more exports. Besides all this there is our large home market. (CoID 1946a)

The Economist (1946), in an important and perceptive leading article on industrial design, drew attention to the fact that, with one or two notable exceptions, there had been comparatively little detailed and systematic research into the realities of design in British industry. Furthermore, in order to demonstrate the economic significance of the CoID's task on the domestic front in the recstruction era, the writer drew attention to the Budget White Papers which showed the expenditure on consumer goods and services in 1938: a quarter of this (£1031 m) was directly attributable to purchases of commodities affected by industrial design; a further very large, but unquantifiable, volume of expenditure on articles involving industrial design was incurred by business, public authorities and other bodies.

An effective and tangible means of tackling the daunting problems that faced the CoID was the organisation of a large-scale exhibition. This would have the added advantage of stimulating public interest in design and creating a showcase for the best British products in the export market. Thus Sir Stafford Cripps, Dalton's successor as President of the Board of Trade of the new Labour Government duly announced, in the autumn of 1945, a national exhibition of Industrial Design, later retitled Britain Can Make It (BCMI) with the rider, 'Good design — and good business'.

An exhibition committee was set up under Sir Thomas Barlow, the first Chairman of the CoID, with representatives from many branches of industry and design: R Dudley Ryder was appointed secretary and manager; James Gardner was called in as designer and Basil Spence as consulting architect. The 1946 exhibition was to occupy 90 000 square feet of the Victoria and Albert Museum, conveniently empty at the time as it had been cleared during the War years.

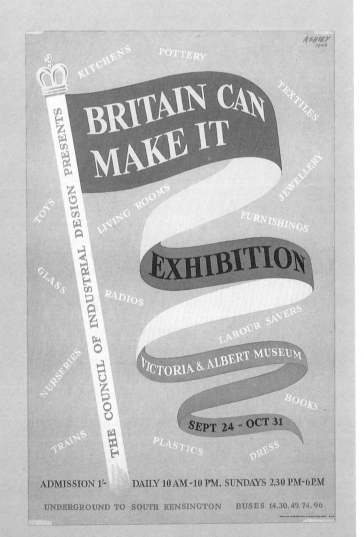

Poster for 'Britain Can Make It', designed by Ashley Havinden, V & A Museum

The displays and settings were often imaginative and witty, and were widely praised. The overall scheme clearly benefited from the organisational experience and techniques developed in wartime propaganda exhibitions. Structured in a logical and informative manner, the exhibition explored the theme of converting wartime production techniques and innovations to peacetime ends in the opening 'From War to Peace' section; this led to a display of 'What the Goods are made of', followed by 'Shopwindow Street' where the importance of imaginative display techniques as an aid to sales was emphasised; and so on through a wide variety of product types and ranges, culminating in the rather forced 'Designers Look Ahead' display. Products shown included domestic appliances, toys, lighting, pottery and glass, kitchenware, bathroom equipment, garden tools and sports equipment, furniture and furnishing fabrics, textiles, fashion and clothing, wallpapers, audio-visual equipment and travel goods.

Owing to shortages of materials and labour, many of the products on display could not be bought. It had been decided to encourage manufacturers to submit goods for selection that were not in quantity production by the time the exhibition opened, as it was felt to be essential for British firms to demonstrate their potential, as well as actual, capability as a potent force in the competitive markets of the post-War era. This gave the popular press a golden opportunity to dub the exhibition 'Britain Can't Have It', an epithet given an extra edge by recurring economic crises and shortages of housing and fuel. It was not, however, the view shared by most serious reviewers of the exhibition: JBB (1946) in *Punch* declared that he found such reports misleading, as he had expected to find most products for export only, but in fact found this to be far from the truth.

Whether or not Britain could 'Get It', BCMI proved a tremendous public success, attracting 1 432 546 visitors — about three or four times the original estimate. The total included over 7000 overseas buyers from 67 countries and at least 43 000 British trade visitors. Another *Punch* reviewer proposed an explanation for the widespread interest, saying:

I'm sure the principal reason is that our eyes have become so accustomed to drab colour and austere cuts that we just haven't been able to resist this post-War opportunity to gaze into a brilliant shop window — as colourful as any of the old Christmas bazaars.

Opened by the King and Queen on 24 September 1946, the exhibition at once attracted considerable crowds. On 26 September, a day on which about 20 000 people visited the exhibition, mounted police were called out to control the queue of several hundreds yards and people were advised to postpone their visits on account of the crush. Strong pressure was mounted in the House of Commons to transfer BCMI to selected provincial centres such as Birmingham or Glasgow, in order to give additional regional impetus to the post-War production drive. A large-scale showcase for Scottish design in industry, 'Enterprise Scotland', was mounted in Edinburgh in 1947. Like BCMI it proved very successful, attracting 456 000 visitors, including 1000 buyers from 28 countries. Originally BCMI had been planned to open only until 31 October; this was then revised to the end of November and again to the end of the year. Such was the continued popular demand to see the exhibition that, from 12 November, it was decided to close the exhibition to the general public on Tuesday and Thursday mornings to enable trade and foreign visitors and others with a professional interest in design to study the exhibits without being overcrowded. MPs were even allocated tickets which allowed them to 'jump the queue'.

One of the most fundamental aims of the CoID was to promote better standards of design in industry and to make available the appropriate advice and information. To this end a series of stage-managed encounters between a 'surrealistically-conceived' visitor and designer punctuated the route into the exhibition. The reviewer from *Punch* (JBB 1946) thought that the majority of people entering BCMI would have felt some uneasiness at being greeted by a Cyclopic figure equipped with a loudspeaker, until they were reassured by the BBC English tones of its message that 'Britain Can Make It'.

The key section in terms of design education was devoted to an explanation of 'What Industrial Design Means'. Designed by Misha Black, the aim was to explain the process involved in solving a particular design problem, in this case the 'Birth of an Egg Cup'. The first part of the display was devoted to the question of 'Who Designs the Egg Cup?' with consideration of the egg producer (the hen), the machinery for manufacture and the industrial designer who, together with factory management, engineers and salespersons, determined the outcome.

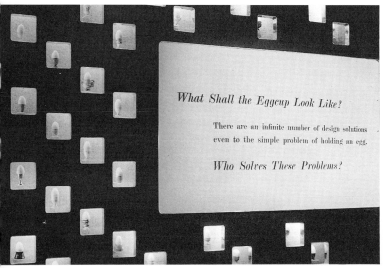

Part of the 'What Industrial Design Means' section designed by Misha Black

The second part examined the ways in which the various materials and methods of manufacture influence the design; and the third dealt with considerations common to any designed object — shape, size, weight, balance, colour, surface treatment and decoration — which, when satisfactorily blended, achieve an aesthetically pleasing and functionally acceptable result.

In some cases manufacturers whose goods were on display also sought to convey something of the design process. For instance, the General Electrical Company (GEC) in its booklet *GEC Products and the Britain Can Make It Exhibition*, analysed photographs of some of its exhibits of light fittings, vacuum cleaners, wall fans, electric cookers, warming plates, toasters and fires in brief synopses explaining the problems that arose during the evolution of the designers as well as the ways in which they were overcome.

Despite the fairly rigorous selection procedures, there clearly was a lack of consistent design standards throughout the exhibition. Some 15 259 products had been put forward for inclusion by 3385 firms from which 5258 items were selected from 1297 firms. This 67% rejection rate led to considerable dissatisfaction among many sectors of manufacturing industry which had, no doubt, submitted what were felt to be their best available designs. As Raymond Mortimer remarked in *The New Statesman & Nation* 'fury is widespread among manufacturers . . . in the Five Towns protest is already shrill' (Mortimer 1946). Despite this indignation many critics felt that there were many weak areas in the exhibition, including those on glass, silver, jewellery and plate. Herbert Read considered in his *Listener* review (Read 1946) that, although there were high standards of design in traditional areas like pottery and textiles, the self-same industries were also responsible for 'the worst designs, bastard descendents of Victorian eclecticism'. Despite finding much to praise at BCMI he was also of the opinion that the exhibition was by no means a fulsome proof of the robust health of British design. Like his fellow reviewer in *The Economist* (1946b) he felt that, due to the short time in which the whole enterprise was mounted, the selectors had 'to accept many articles of inferior, even of outrageously bad, design'. This did not necessarily help the cause of the CoID which was entirely responsible for the selection of all exhibits — manufacturers were unable to buy space at BCMI as was their practice at trade fairs. The Council had stated in its Plan and Policy paper for BCMI that the

. . . selection of goods will be made by expert committees, whose members will between them possess, not only authority, as judges of design, but knowledge of the technical problems and processes of the industries concerned and of the commercial and marketing questions with which they have to deal. (CoID 1945)

But, despite its avowed intention to accept no bad designs, the Council itself admitted in its *Annual Report* of 1946/47 that, although the standards of display and presentation were widely admired, 'the reaction to the standard of exhibits, especially on the part of overseas buyers and commentators, was less whole hearted'. (CoID 1947)

This lack of consistent and rigorous criteria for the Council's selection of products for display in exhibitions (or, as later, for inclusion in the Design Index) was the cause of continued criticism, both on grounds of aesthetics and product performance. In the late 1940s, as the Board of Trade eased its guidelines and stringent specifications for many categories of goods produced under the Utility Label, there were many campaigns afoot to ensure that the consumer should continue to be able to expect adequate safeguards in product standards and value for money in the design of consumer goods in the post-War period. Hilde Marchant, writing in *Picture Post* in 1948, typified this widespread concern when she declared that, while there was 'a chance for inferior work getting on the market, the good name of British products will suffer' (Marchant 1948). By way of supportive illustration a number of photographs of shoddy goods accompanied the text, exemplified by such examples as 'The strainer that does not strain', 'The vegetable masher that didn't' and 'Footwear that won't'. In such a climate it was clear that the everyday consumer was at least as concerned with practicality and durability as with aesthetic prerequisites of good design. Although the CoID used all three concerns as criteria for the selection of goods, it was not at all clear how the lay person could ascertain whether a product was 'honestly made to withstand wear and tear' or could 'do the job it is made for' without access to informed and systematic modes of testing or the resultant findings.

A member of the ceramic section of the Britain Can Make It selection committee at work

Throughout the 1950s further questions were asked about the nature of the criteria used for the selection of goods for the Design Index, for display in The Design Centre after its opening in 1956, for the Design Centre Awards scheme initiated in 1957, and for the labelling scheme launched in 1959. A number of critics became increasingly concerned that CoID-approved products should be safe and practical to use as well as looking good. Katherine Whitehorn, writing in *The Spectator* in 1960, declared that 'no-one wants to see the design awards handed out simply on the score of practicality' but that the CoID 'might do worse than behave like the Légion d'Honneur who, before bestowing the honour, have the police do a few checks first'. Reyner Banham, writing for *The New Statesman* in the following year, drew attention to the fact that that the Council had no facilities for quality testing and relied on the 'X-ray eyes' of the selection panels rather than on the accumulated experience of the Industrial Officers. Soon afterwards *Punch* ran three pages on The Design Centre (demonstrating its topicality at least). One cartoon neatly encapsulated the conflict of aesthetics and practicality: a wife chides her husband who is struggling to control their five children, saying 'I'm looking for an elegant design. Why do you keep harping on strength and durability?'

All such comments should be viewed against a background of improving consumer protection and awareness in Britain. The British Standards Institution set up the Advisory Council on Standards for Consumer Goods, and the Consumers' Association launched *Shopper's Guide* and *Which?* in 1957. Examples were cited of products that had been singled out in the consumer press as poorly designed, in terms of intended function, durability and practicality, but which were approved by the CoID selection panels and featured in the Design Index. It was no longer tenable for writers such as Kenneth Robinson, in *Design* magazine, to defend the efficacy of the Council's procedures in a merely negative fashion, by implying that most criticisms were simply unreasonable. He wanted his public to be wary of

the man who will tell you that a table in The Design Centre is too easily scratched, that a tea pot shown won't pour and that a garden spade on view is likely to break in half. Before you reply, search him for sharp objects, take his finger out of the spout and have a look at the concrete foundations of his flower bed. (Robinson 1958)

The Molony committee's *Final Report on Consumer Protection* for the Board of Trade in 1962 was heavily critical of many organisations purporting to give consumer advice on product reliability. It recognised the Council as an effective propagandist for better aesthetic standards of design, through The Design Centre, Design Index and its labelling scheme. However, it also roundly criticised it for its lack of testing standards relating to product efficiency, durability and value for money.

Another closely related problem that confronted the Council, both at BCMI and afterwards, concerned the difference between the aesthetic of the approved products and the design values espoused by different social groups. This opposition of values was to become more contentious as the influence of the Council became more apparent, providing ammunition for less than friendly critics for a number of years: John Berger cast the CoID in the role of advocate of middle-class values; Reyner Banham remarked in 1961 that The Design Centre was reflective of an official aesthetic, 'HM Fashion House'; Mahood, in a *Punch* cartoon, portrayed two women looking at a chair in The Design Centre, with one saying to the other, 'You may be right about the design but I would want to see how Ena Sharples looks in it before I decided.'

One section at BCMI that especially revealed the more prescriptive side of the CoID aesthetic was the Furnished Rooms. The idea of furnished rooms as a means of design promotion in the public eye had long been used, both at home and abroad. It was, however, generally agreed that the 1946 settings showed a greater sense of social awareness than had their predecessors in the design propaganda shows of the 1930s. It was a method that the Council continued to explore after 1946, at the Ideal Homes exhibition and elsewhere. At BCMI itself an extensive range of specific room settings designed for a wide range of fictitious families from almost all income groups were exhibited. The catalogue entries were accompanied by line drawings by Nicolas Bentley, characterising the imagined families 'living' in the rooms, and textual vignettes by John Betjeman. For the Kitchen of a Cottage in a Modern Mining Village by Edna Moseley the caption read: 'THE FAMILY: Coal miner, middle-aged, active trade unionist, member of a colliery choir. His wife, a member of Women's Institute; their three children.' From this end of the spectrum one could move to A Kitchen in a well-appointed House designed by Maxwell Fry and Jane Drew with its caption: 'THE FAMILY: Managing director of an engineering works; university education. His wife; lived in America for some years. Their daughter, now at boarding school. Their staff; two maids and a manservant.' However, some reviewers felt that there was an almost puritanical atmosphere exuding from the Furnished Rooms display. As the *Picture Post* reviewer remarked,

. . . in the welter of stripes and spots and whitewood and home-spun it would have been almost a relief to see a vast chintzy armchair . . . design has yet to fit comfortably into the British home. (*Picture Post* 1946)

In the leading article published three days before BCMI opened *The Economist* (1946a) stressed the need for a recognition of the sociology of design, suggesting that general public affection for highly decorated and ostentatious design was due to a collective wish to establish a

Edna Moseley's Kitchen of a cottage in a Modern Mining Village

domestic environment, which contrasted markedly with the general austerity and unwelcoming atmosphere of their place of work. Five years later the *Architectural Review* was rather more censorious. It felt that the CoID should be seen to devote its energies to the promotion of good design rather attempting to control it, since the latter might lead to a reaction against its design ideals. Furthermore the importance of individual preference was emphasised:

> You must be allowed the savoyard boy on the cill of your bay-window or the lamp with a lady in an irridescent turquoise frock dancing a tarantella, or even a multi-coloured printed tie — as long as you like them. (*Architectural Review* 1951)

Herbert Read, writing in the context of BCMI in 1946, also recognised problems relating to public taste in an age of 'dehumanised' mass production. His view was that public taste had evolved from a tradition centred on manual skills, themselves fostered by the apprentice system. These had been replaced by machine-based skills which had no naturally inherited place in society, were out of key with family life and precluded a genuine involvement with work and a natural understanding of materials.

For many years individuals and organisations concerned with improving standards of design in British industry had considered that the problem was fundamentally an educational one, campaigning for the initiation of design awareness programmes as part of the school curriculum from an early stage. S B L Jacks of R Greg & Co certainly felt so after walking round BCMI, listening to the comments of the general public. He related his experience thus:

My own firm had taken part in the manufacture of a particularly lovely design which had been well commented upon by many designers. I finally ran it to ground as the backing for a chair in the rest-lounge. Sitting on that chair was a gentleman of about thirty-five and I said to him: 'I wonder if you would mind moving, sir?' He said 'I shall be delighted' and he got up, and I said: 'Now, what do you think, sir?'. 'Well,' he said, 'I'm damned. If I had known it was as awful as that I should never have sat on it'. (CoID 1946b)

In addition to the introductory section, the 'What Industrial Design Means' display and the numerous official publications, the Council sought to engender a sense of critical awareness in the general public by the organisation of a Design Quiz. On their way into the exhibition the visitors passed a quiz stall where they were issued with a bag containing plastic coins for placing in a series of ten quiz banks, situated at various points throughout the exhibition. These quiz banks consisted of three mounted photographs of different designs for a single product type, located above three corresponding slots into which, after due consideration of the CoID's hints on efficiency, materials and appearance, visitors could indicate their particular penchant. The practice of taste-testing, a staple ingredient in today's magazine competitions, was well established by this time. The CoID itself had already tried it out at the *Daily Herald* Post-War Homes exhibition in the summer of 1945. The popular appeal of such a venture may be gleaned from the fact that the Council mounted another design quiz stand at the *Daily Herald* Modern Homes exhibition at Dorland Hall in the following March; in the late 1940s the Council produced a 17 shilling wall-card design quiz as a teaching aid.

Buyers and retailers had long been cast by those campaigning for better standards of design as the arch conspirators in the plot to frustrate their untiring efforts. Naturally, the CoID sought to engage their attention at BCMI: at least 43 000 British trade visitors and 7000 overseas buyers came to the exhibition. The Council was not alone in addressing this sector of the public. Raymond Mortimer, in his review in *The New Statesman & Nation*, made a specific plea to the authorities of the Co-operative Wholesale Society, declaring that

. . . no other body can do so much to improve or debase public taste — and hitherto their influence has not been fortunate. If they would accept the standards and advice of the Council of Industrial Design, the benefit to the country would be inestimable. (Mortimer 1946)

The CoID tried to stimulate an interest in design within the Co-operative movement, working closely with the education department of the Co-operative Union Ltd from 1950 onwards. As well as launching courses, lectures and summer schools for the Co-operative movement, the Council produced with it a joint booklet entitled *Design and Our Homes*; in December 1955 another joint booklet, *Colour and Pattern in Your Home*, was issued with an initial print run of 100 000.

The Council's activities directed towards the retail trade were fairly diverse in the wake of BCMI. In 1947 a programme of Design Weeks — a CoID roadshow — was initiated in a number of provincial centres, starting with Newcastle-upon-Tyne. The Council, the FBI and the Association of British Chambers of Commerce organised conferences of manufacturers and retailers. This set the scene for a continuing programme of courses for retail staff and customers, reinvigorated by the Festival of Britain in 1951.

The opening of The Design Centre in Haymarket in 1956 afforded the Council a further golden opportunity to liaise with retailers and buying houses. Over 100 retail outlets throughout Britain put on special window displays to coincide with the event and many more asked to be circulated with the quarterly lists of approved products. It was also established, in a survey carried out in the first year of the Centre's existence, that 10% of its visitors were trade buyers of some sort. Further concerted liaison with the retail sector came with the launch of The Design Centre labelling scheme in 1959, publicised in window displays in 81 shops throughout the country.

A drawing by David Knight showing an impression of the interior of the Design Centre at Haymarket House before it opened in April 1956

The somewhat uneasy balance between the capital goods (engineering) and industrial design sectors of the Council was perhaps foreshadowed by events relating to the Transport section, originally planned as part of the BCMI exhibition. On 14 June 1946 the Council decided to cancel the Transport section (comprising coach, wagon, ship and aircraft interiors and motor bodies) which would have occupied a substantial part of the exhibition space — about 7% (6300 square feet). Although the motor industry had expressed a willingness to participate in the venture, it devoted its major energies to the export drive and, largely due to the prevailing market conditions, was unable to produce and display models embracing genuinely new designs; the shipping industry also was unable to present new ideas, nor was it possible to produce a full-scale model of a post-War civil aircraft as had been hoped. Since only the railway companies were prepared, the decision was made to cancel the section. This omission from BCMI was something which was reflected in the Council's activities for many years to come.

The Council had an important part to play in the educational sector: in 1946, as a counterpart to BCMI, it organised with the FBI a conference on industrial design. In the same year it published its report on *The Training of the Industrial Designer in England and Wales*; it also began to involve itself in the education of younger people. Over 160 000 visitors to BCMI were schoolchildren. The Council was concerned with design awareness at elementary and secondary level on the grounds that schoolchildren were to be the future consumers of industrial design. From an early stage of its existence the Council had attempted to reach schoolchildren, through collaboration with the Ministry of Education, local authorities, museums and others, and the circulation of a monthly series of *Design Folios*. These were designed for teaching purposes and consisted of introductory essays with illustrations, focusing on a variety of design products. One of the most fruitful educational liaisons was with the LCC. Jointly organised exhibitions were circulated to secondary schools and teacher-training colleges, and provided a source of inspiration to other authorities. In the mid-1950s the Council also collaborated with the BBC in a series on design appreciation for children. Other opportunities arose with the opening of The Design Centre in 1956: 75% (351) of the group visits made to the Centre in its first year were school parties. The Design Council has maintained and developed such links with the secondary (as well as tertiary) sector through its Education Advisory Committee and Secondary Education Subcommittee.

One of the most difficult tasks facing the CoID in 1946 concerned the relative ineffectiveness of design education in Britain. Similar contemporary concerns were voiced in a fascinating and revealing correspondence in *The Times* during January 1945, shortly after the CoID had been set up. Herbert Read, ever ready with his pen, lamented the almost complete absence of design training relating to machine tools and mass production; also the lack of the staff and equipment necessary to initiate such a training. He concluded by expressing doubt that there were more than about a dozen people in Britain who were sufficiently competent to become consultant designers in British industry. Although rather sweeping, such a view reflected the call for industrial re-orientation which Weir had recommended for the Royal College of Art: studies devoted to the economics of design, factory placements, fully-equipped workshops, practising designers as teachers and the renaming of the institution as the Royal College of Art and Design. Meynell-Hoskin suggested the more radical retitling of Royal College of Design.

Since its inception, the CoID has had a continuing and important involvement in the debates on design education. In 1946 it published its report on *The Training of the Industrial Designer in England and Wales*, in which it hoped to reassure manufacturers of its businesslike intent by challenging fine art as the dictating force in British visual arts education. It also advocated collaboration between art schools and technical colleges. This educational commitment has continued, seen more recently in the Carter Report on *Industrial Design in the United Kingdom*, the Hayes Report on *The Industrial Design Requirements of Industry*, the Design Management Development Project and the Curriculum Development Scheme. However, the Design Council itself, through its publication *Engineering Design Education*, appears to feel that there is still much to achieve. Commenting on the recent reorganisation within the RCA, the view was embraced that,

> . . . productivity, cost-effectiveness and a grasp of high technology must be achieved if the UK is to survive in a climate of desperate international competition. Whilst this message has been present in design education . . . this is the first time the message has been imposed forcefully and prominently in the sheltered world of art and design education in the UK. . . . The issue that the RCA is facing is the fundamental difference between fine art and design — the argument involving 'art for art's sake' and 'design for profit'.
> (Design Council 1985)

Since 1946, a time of economic uncertainty and initiatives in design education, the wheel has turned full circle.

What of manufacturing industry itself? As indicated earlier, CoID propaganda aimed at British manufacturers in 1946 was not solely restricted to BCMI or the activities of the selection committees. The Council, together with the FBI, mounted a conference about industrial design three days after the opening of the exhibition. Attention was devoted to themes which related to design in the context of the post-War export drive: industry and the designer, design for machinery, humanising industrial design, design selling, design training and others. Such topics had preoccupied design-related bodies throughout the history of British design for the mass-market, especially during the inter-War period. Pevsner, in his 1937 *Enquiry into Industrial Art in England*, had established the widespread poverty of design awareness in British industry and the Council for Art and Industry's report of the same year, *Design and the Designer in British Industry*, confirmed the lowly status, prospects and salary of the British designer. Such was the legacy which the CoID inherited and sought to overcome in the ensuing decades. At BCMI, just as at the British Art in Industry exhibition of 1935, attempts were made to enhance the status of the designer in the public eye by displaying his or her name alongside the manufacturer in the catalogue and elsewhere. But a major problem was that, despite the existence of the Society of Industrial Artists (SIA), the designer had no real professional standing on a par with, for example, architects. At the 1946 CoID–FBI conference, Josiah Wedgwood called for the recognition of the chief designer in industry as

. . . a key executive and expert in his own field. Therefore he must be accorded the same status and respect as other key executives and experts in other fields — that means something more than good pay and a decent studio or drawing office . . . it is no exaggeration to say that at the present time in many businesses the designer is just used as a draughtsman for sales staff. (CoID 1946b)

The same theme was still being explored five years later at the CoID-sponsored Design Congress held at the RCA. Entitled 'Design policy in industry as a responsibility of high level management', it attracted eminent speakers and delegates from overseas as well as representatives from the FBI, SIA, RCA, the Trades Union Congress and the Royal Society of Arts. It led to the publication of the Council booklet on *Design Policy in Industry*. In 1956 a further CoID Design Congress was mounted on the main theme of 'The Management of design; or the integration of the designer with management'.

The fact that we are still concerned with debates and reports on the role of design in the British economy, the industrial requirements of industry and the development of design management, is perhaps a reflection of the resurgent emphasis on design as a marketing tool in times of economic difficulty. The relative failure of British manufacturing industry to address itself sufficiently to such problems is perhaps a measure of the comparatively barren soil upon which the CoID, later the Design Council, has had to sow its propagandist seed since the days of Britain Can Make It.

REFERENCES

Banham, R (1961) 'H. M. Fashion House', *The New Statesman*, 27 January, pp 151/152.

Council for Art and Industry (1937) *Design and the Designer*, HMSO.

CoID (1946a) *Annual Report 1945/46*.

CoID (1946b) *Conference on Industrial Design*.

CoID (1945) *Preliminary Notice* for 'Britain Can Make It'.

CoID (1947) *Annual Report 1946/47*.

Design Council (1985) 'Turner or Technology' *Engineering Design Education*, Spring, p 52.

Economist, The (1946) 'Industrial Design' 21 September, pp 445/446.

GEC (1946) *GEC Products and the Britain Can Make It Exhibition*, GEC.

JBB (1946) 'Britain Can Make It: A Late Look Round' *Punch*, 30 October, pp 374/375.

Marchant, H (1948) 'It's Time This Shoddiness Ended', *Picture Post*, 24 July, pp 7/9.

Mortimer, R (1946) 'Britain Can Make It!' *The New Statesman & Nation*, 28 September, p 220.

Molony Committee (1962) *Final Report on Consumer Protection*, HMSO.

Pevsner, N (1937) *An Enquiry into Industrial Art in England*, Cambridge University.

Picture Post (1946) 'Britain Can Make It', 19 October, pp 21/23.

Punch (1946) 'The Great Exhibition', 16 October, p 305.

Read, H (1946) 'Britain Can Make It' *The Listener*, 3 October, pp 429/430.

Robinson, K (1958) 'It came apart in me 'and', *Design*, December, p 26.

Whitehorn, K (1960) 'Intents and Purposes' *The Spectator*, 20 May, p 749.

Poster designed by Hans Schleger
advertising the Design Centre, 1956–57

JONATHAN M WOODHAM INTERVIEWS LORD REILLY

WOODHAM

As you know, at the Britain Can Make It exhibition of 1946, the Council of Industrial Design hoped to further its original aims: to convince manufacturers of the importance of industrial design; to stimulate design awareness in the British public; and to act as a shopwindow for British industrial design in international markets. In general, how successful do you think the Council has been in realising these aims over the last 40 years?

REILLY

Manufacturers today are certainly more aware of the word 'design' than when I was at the Council. But the public certainly need a lot more persuasion.

In what way?

If you walk down any High Street you will see what I mean. Do you know Putney High Street? Walking down Putney High Street makes you wonder what the Design Council has been up to all these years.

What about the Council's role as an international shopwindow?

In the 50s and 60s it was very good, less so today. In fact, I'm rather worried about standards of design in Britain. Although there has been some improvement in the quality of domestic appliances their aesthetics are still fairly poor.

Perhaps we can pick up some of these issues again later on . . . In Britain today, just as in the economically unsettled 1940s, a great deal of energy is being expended on debates about greater industrial orientation in design education, effective design representation at boardroom level, and the promotion of design as a 'key function in the commercial exploitation of goods'.

There is a lot of energy and a lot of people trying very hard.

Does this tell us anything about manufacturing and business attitudes to design and the economy in the post-War period?

Do you ever go to Harrods? It's ghastly and geared to Americans who pin us to our past. That's the nature of the problem.

When you were Information Officer at the Council in the 1950s, did you think that you were making headway in the promotion of better standards of design in British industry?

I can hardly remember, it's such a long time ago. Of course the Festival of Britain was very important.

*Occasional chair
and table design
by A J Milne for
Heals in 1953
showing splayed
legs typical of the
period*

Although some critics, as in the Architectural Review, *felt that
quite a number of exhibits on show on the South Bank were far
from being examples of good design.*

I don't agree, especially if you compare them with what was in the
shops at the time. Designers certainly choose much better than the
ordinary man in the street but splayed legs were fairly tiresome I think.

*Other than the Festival what do you think were the most effective
means of promoting better standards of design in British industry
— Design magazine, for example?*

It's not so useful today. For the past year or so it's been an example
of straight bad design typographically, with the underlining of sentences
and so on.

*It was also criticised in the 50s as not representing the best of British
typography.*

It was certainly much better in the 1950s and 60s.

Was it more important then than it is now?

Yes. Now it's expensive, its circulation has fallen and it has been poor
over the past year or two. I wonder who reads it . . .?

*How far do you think that the level of grant allocation to the
Council has restricted or advanced its activities? There have been
times, as in the early 1950s, when funding has been fairly ungen-
erous, leading to difficulties such as the lack of official backing for
the British contribution to the important international exhibition at
Halsingborg in 1955.*

We put on rather a good display at Halsingborg. It was well thought
of and successful.

But it was only after Sir Kenneth Lee appealed in The Times
*for funding from private industry that the Council was able to
participate.*

Kenneth Lee was a good member of the Council.

Were there many funding problems while you were at the Council?
All the time. Funding has always been bad. I always remember the annual battle with the Board of Trade, later Trade and Industry. Sympathy always depended on the level of person you were dealing with. If you were talking to a junior you got a frightened answer, to a senior something quite different. Some of the First Permanent Secretaries were excellent, and still are.

How much influence do you feel that the Design Council has brought to bear on the development of British design education?
It's had little influence on design education — certainly not until the late 60s when it got to the secondary schools. I remember a story concerned with the British Weeks in Sweden, Mrs Thatcher was over there as an Opposition MP as part of a delegation to see what the British Weeks were like. She was with Lord Peddie from the Labour Party and a Peer from the Liberal Party. She was absolutely furious about the shopwindow displays and threatened to kick up a fuss on her return.

What were they?
The Swedish shops backed British Week by mounting displays of what they thought was most British. They were absolutely ghastly. It's surprising that the Swedes should choose examples like repro Jaco — some people even measured the success of British Weeks with the number of shopwindows showing such rubbish. Anyway, I asked Mrs Thatcher if she'd seen the two main exhibitions, one partly paid for by the Board of Trade, the other by the Swedish Co-operative Society. She hadn't. She told me then that she felt that the Council would never achieve its aims unless it won the battle in the classrooms. Soon afterwards she was made Secretary of State for Education and so I wrote to her, reminding her of her remarks, and she invited me to discuss the problem with her . . . She had soon discovered that as Minister she had no power to put anything right. She proposed a sandwich lunch for Head Masters and Mistresses from Secondary Schools, and she and I would talk to them. She firmly believed that one could encourage children to look, to use their eyes. (I was introduced to design in this way at prep school. My geography and history teachers used illustrations and photographs of architecture, clothing and objects wherever possible.) However, the Head Masters and Mistresses said we were wrong — they said that children must use their hands.

Why?
It was a vogue — the wheel of fashion pointing to handwork as the solution.

To go back for a moment to your early interest in design — presumably your father, Sir Charles Reilly, the architect, was an important influence?
He was a great figure in my life. My grandfather too. He commissioned William Morris for carpets in the Drapers Hall. The two men I owe most to are Gordon Russell and my father.

In terms of design education, the Council did develop some interesting projects with LCC secondary schools and teacher training colleges in the 1950s.

They were very good indeed, a step in the right direction.

And that was at a time when the Council was very poorly funded.

With a good idea one can generate money.

More recently there have been a lot of Design Council reports relating to education.

There have. The new Director is a good administrator.

British design education has been, and often is, blamed by industry and others for its lack of realism and relevance to contemporary needs. Since a large number of British-trained designers have been, and are, employed by many of our foreign competitors how far do you think it fair to blame the British educational system?

Things are better today than for a long while. But there are too many teachers who are afraid of industry and industralists haven't the time to get to know teachers. So a gap still exists. It's not through ill-will, it's just a matter of time.

Are our competitors better than us?

Have you read the report in today's *Times*[1] on the NEDO survey on domestic appliance design which shows that British is the best in Europe?

Isn't that more concerned with performance than aesthetics?

It's still a better overall picture.

Although the promotion of British design has been a central feature of the Design Council's philosophy, wouldn't the Council have further heightened manufacturers' awareness of the possibilities and economic benefits of well designed products by making them more aware of some of the achievements of our competitors, something that to an extent, at least originally, the V & A Boilerhouse Project set out to do in 1982?

I don't think that the Boilerhouse achieved very much in that first exhibition on Art and Industry. But the Design Council has, I think, done what you are suggesting, as in the 'Designed in Britain — Made Abroad' exhibition a few years ago.

That was about British designers working for foreign firms. Are they the best examples of foreign competition?

They were very good examples.

Is Design *magazine a good means of introducing people to our foreign competitors?*

Design goes up and down over the years. If you pick any one-year or five-year spell it can be very good, then it dips.

What do you feel were the main difficulties facing the Council when you succeeded Sir Gordon Russell as Director in 1960?

Things were not good enough and are still not. I'm talking about objects.

Interior of the Boilerhouse in the Victoria & Albert Museum, showing the 'Art and Industry' exhibition in 1982

Was the administrative machinery and organisation good?
Yes. Everything was good. I enjoyed my time at the Council . . . I've no real criticism. Of course, soon after Gordon left Tony Snowdon arrived and that 'set the cat among the pigeons'.

You mean it didn't go down well with people like Reyner Banham?
Reyner Banham and a man who used to work for the Council: Kenneth Robinson. They were the two most persistent critics. I never took Reyner Banham seriously, clever man that he is. He never knew what generation he belonged to. Robinson kept chipping away, year after year. I think he's given up now.

I think he's fairly critical of anything he reviews. Of course in the late 1950s and early 60s the Council did come under a fair amount of criticism from several quarters. Accusations were made that the Council endorsed 'middle-class values'.
Inevitably. If you have a clear idea what is right you are bound to quarrel with many people. I remember showing Aneurin Bevan round a furnished house at the Ideal Homes Exhibition. He said that he thought that the Council was quite right in furnishing in middle-class taste since the working classes never seem to get it out of their heads that the middle class know better than they do how to spend money wisely. We wanted to improve everything. Of course, today working-class values rate more highly than they did in the 1950s and 60s. I'm not quite sure what you're trying to say.

I meant that critics like Alloway, Banham and others were saying that the aesthetics of Berenson, Fry or Read were no longer relevant to the fast-changing post-War world which accepted obsolescence as part of everyday life. Banham saw styling of products as 'the common man's toehold on technology', as in the tail-fins on 50s American cars.

How wrong Banham was — look what's happened to his fins.

People also said that the Council was more concerned with the appearance of products than their performance, safety and practicality, as in the Molony Report.

It's strange, but I don't really remember the Report. But we did cross-link with the Consumers' Association. When I took the Council into engineering we couldn't go wrong. The first major activity was in the 1958 Birmingham conference on 'Industrial Design and the Engineering Industries', organised by the Council with an audience of engineers. Then we appointed an engineer to the staff. He didn't stay long and became managing director of a famous, and rather awful, furniture firm. We replaced him with Bill Mayall which was much more successful.

What about the criticisms about lack of product testing? Did someone just take the products home and try them out?

Of course we weren't so foolish as to simply take them home and try them out. We did have a system, although I can't remember now exactly how it worked. I do remember though, that we got into trouble with an electric razor which won the Duke of Edinburgh's Elegant Design Prize. A writer in one of the Sunday papers said that it didn't work properly as it left some hairs in his beard. The Duke of Edinburgh said 'Has he not got a pair of nail scissors to trim them?'

In 1979 you said of your latter days at the Council: 'I began to find myself out of touch and indeed out of sympathy with some of the most popular and to me most frivolous manifestations of modern design'. Perhaps you could clarify this?

Appearance must be high in any classification of design. The Design Centre began to be filled with a lot of things I didn't like, such as padded clothes hangers.

You mean that it became very commercialised? Is that a bad thing?

Commercialism is a good thing if they do it better than anyone else in the country. But I don't think that they do. When I started the excellent bookshop I wanted to make sure that everything in the bookshop illustrated good design. Now it sells absolutely anything.

What are the main differences between the Council under your Directorship and the organisation as it operates today?

Style.

In terms of organisation or objects?

Everything. Style is quality in the sense I was meaning it.

What about the bringing together of industrial design and engineering? Has that worked?

Yes, the marriage is a happy one . . . the engineers have a very strong voice. Terence Conran resigned from the Council when it changed its name; he said that the 'engineers will swamp you'. I don't think they have, but I can see his worry.

What do you look back on with greatest satisfaction in your period
as Director?

World travel. I went to all five continents, always taking exhibitions which were very good, I must say. I was very happy there. I enjoyed myself, that's the trouble.

Tea cosy and egg cosy from Brendatoys on
sale at The Design Centre in 1981

1. *The Times*, 9 August 1985, pp 3, 11.

Part 3

The Professional Designer

Moving on from the role of the Design Council to that of the designer himself, this part examines the way in which the professional freelance designer, and the design team, have evolved during the post War period. The two chapters focus on different aspects of this evolution; the first, written by myself, concentrates on the career of the freelance graphic designer Abram Games, who, in choosing to set himself up alone back in the 1930s, took an important step forward. His greatest opportunity came, however, during his years in the army in the Second World War. The second part, by way of a contrast, is the story of the British design team in the years between 1946 and 1982, narrated by one of its participants, Wally Olins of the Wolff Olins design consultancy. Based primarily upon memory and personal involvement, this second chapter assesses the international significance of the British design consultant and shows how the evolution of this phenomenon is one of Britain's most notable post War achievements.

ABRAM GAMES: FREELANCE GRAPHIC DESIGNER IN THE 1940s AND 50s
PENNY SPARKE

Abram Games set himself up as an independent graphic designer in 1935. In any discussion of the so-called 'design profession' in Britain since the war, it is vital to stress the role that two-dimensional designers played in the early years of its establishment. Back in the 1930s, before the term 'designer' came into general usage and when the 'commercial artist' was a much better known concept, the role of the two-dimensional artist was of fundamental importance: it was he, for instance, who, long before art school industrial designers were let loose on the products of the new technological age, drew the pictures of sewing-machines, ladies' stockings and corsets which were used in the catalogues and brochures advertising those products.

The commercial artist was the main link between manufacturing industry and sales at this time, while the design of the products themselves was left mostly to in-house, anonymous, specialist craftsmen and engineers, all of whom influenced the way things looked but who had precious few links with the world of commerce. Advertising agencies filled this gap and commissioned work from the most talented graphic artists of the day, who succeeded in building up a reputation for British two-dimensional design in these years. Large companies such as Shell, the Post Office and London Transport acted as design patrons, sponsoring information and publicity programmes that brought in work from the 'big names' of the day, among them E McKnight Kauffer, Tom Purvis, Arthur Cooper, Edward Bawden, Hans Schleger, Ashley Havinden, Tom Eckersley, James Fitton, Milner Gray, F H K Henrion and Abram Games, several of whom were emigrés from Europe.

Games had seen the work of, and was hugely influenced by, the most outstanding of them all — Kauffer — during his only two terms of full-time art education, at St Martin's School of Art in 1930. From there he went on, in 1932, to work for a commercial art studio in Fleet Street where he rapidly became disenchanted with the routine work that occupied most of his time there. After a row with his boss he was sacked and subsequently, in his words, 'I made up my mind never to be employed again and to become a freelance.'

This proved to be a major decision which has influenced his entire professional career. In contrast to Misha Black and Milner Gray, who, in 1944, set up the Design Research Unit — the first independent design consultancy in Britain — and Henrion, who, with his background in textiles, diversified in the 1940s and established a 'design business' with a team of assistants, Games decided to practise completely alone, alongside the larger-scale commercial design profession. In many ways Games has retained the self-image of a fine artist, a quality he shares with other notable designers for industry from the 1930s, such as Eric Ravilious (ceramics); Keith Murray (ceramics and glass); Barnett Freedman (graphics); and McKnight Kauffer himself. Describing these men the design propagandist Noel Carrington has remarked that 'these were not artists who would have easily slotted into a partnership.'

From the mid 1930s Games spent a great deal of time seeking work from the 'design patrons' of the day, the large companies which were increasingly aware of the need to bring in outside artists to work on their publicity, and the advertising agencies. The best advice he was given at this time came from Ashley Havinden, whom he visited at Crawfords, and who (although unable to employ him) suggested to Games that he should use a card with his achievements to date printed on it (including his first prize in a London County Council poster competition) and send it to a few potential clients. Through Havinden also, Games was introduced to F A Mercer, editor of *Art and Industry* and, in 1937, was given a double page spread in that magazine. Games sent copies of the issue to 50 possible clients, and from that initiative his first and subsequent poster commissions came in. On the basis of these Games comments, 'I began to build up a freelance practice and found that I was very very busy. I had a little wooden studio built in the garden of my house in Hackney and I worked very happily there.' His best known commercial poster from this period was his 'Bucking Bronco' for Shell which earned him the unprecedented fee of a hundred guineas.

Abram Games 'Bucking Bronco' poster for Shell 1939 (Courtesy of Abram Games)

Games' pre-War experience was representative of the way in which a number of other individuals, including Tom Eckersley, penetrated the professional practice of design at this time. Getting work entailed pursuing a fairly aggressive policy of going out to find it. As yet the freelance designer was a largely unknown quantity and, with only a few notable exceptions, manufacturers were generally reticent about engaging their services. The special circumstances provided by the War, however, opened up unexpected opportunities for many such designers.

ATS recruitment poster, 1941

The main agent for this was the Ministry of Information, which was created in 1939 as a mainly domestic propaganda body. It employed a number of designers in its ranks, including Milner Gray, Misha Black and Reginald Mount. Other designers, notably James Gardner, Ashley Havinden and Richard Gyatt, applied their skills to camouflage for the War effort.

In 1940, Abram Games went into the army and it was there that he was given his greatest opportunity. He recounts that there was an element of luck in the way the War Office selected him to design recruiting posters. Games was the first professional designer whose name a certain Colonel Edgeworth Johnstone came across in the file index. (Games has pointed out that if Eckersley had been in the army he would undoubtedly have been given the job.) Games' new work meant leaving his infantry unit and working in a small room in the War Office. During his early period there he designed his now famous recruitment poster for the ATS, the result of a chance encounter with an attractive young girl who came into his studio asking Games to design a poster for the WO social club. The glamorous treatment of the ATS girl in his poster proved highly provocative and Games recalls that 'It was the subject of controversy in parliament for nearly a month while the Germans were lobbing shells into Dover and there were air raids over the whole country.'

At the suggestion of Jack Beddington, late of Shell and, in 1940, at the Ministry of Information, Games wrote an anonymous memorandum on the use of poster designers in the army. He outlined many vital subjects to be covered by well designed posters: nothing more was heard following Beddington's submission of the document to the War Office. It was solely due to Games' presence there months later that he was able to refer to it and to have it re-examined — announcing himself as its author. He was given a totally free hand to apply its policies and began work immediately on a series of posters (amounting finally to about 100) which focused on a range of subjects such as foot hygiene, VD and ventilation in the barracks. From here he went on to work on the security posters, like 'Your Talk May Kill Your Comrades' and a whole series on anti-gossip, anti-waste, growing your own food, and so forth.

Games was unique in many ways, not only in finally being appointed the only War Office official poster designer, but also in applying the skills he had developed as a freelance designer in the 1930s to the needs of the army during wartime. He also evolved a very special, concise, visual language for the poster which depended utterly on what he has described as 'maximum meaning, minimum means'. His job provided the necessary freedom of operation that he needed to develop this sophisticated means of communication and the army performed the role of a receptive, even an enlightened, client or patron, ever eager to use his latest design: it was a unique situation which was not to last.

Nevertheless the transition from war to peace proved to be a fertile period for Games as he devoted his energies, in the months before he was demobbed, to designing posters for the Army Education Corps — suggesting ways in which soldiers could adapt themselves to civilian life. It was a continuation of the wartime campaign with a subtle shift of emphasis, and posters like 'Serve as a Soldier, Vote as a Citizen' — which was exhibited, along with 'Your Talk may Kill', at Britain Can Make It — emerged in this period. Others concerned with themes such as giving blood and National Savings (for the Ministry of Information at the end of the war) were directed completely at a civilian market. Games was also involved with designing some display panels for a number of MoI exhibitions. It was the nearest he was to come to exhibition design as he felt, and still feels, that there is a completely different intellectual and creative process involved in designing a poster and an exhibition: the former, he maintains, concentrates on the essential message while the other expands outwards. For this reason he did not play a part in the mounting of Britain Can Make It, although he recalls having lunch with a group of the participants and being asked to join them. By then Milner Gray and Misha Black had formed the Design Research Unit and Henrion had branched out into product design and set up his business in London. People like Richard Lonsdale-Hands, Gaby Schreiber and Hulme Chadwick were working directly with what little manufacturing industry was operating at this time and there was a general feeling in the air that the freelance product designer had arrived, modelled largely on the American model of the previous decade. This was reinforced by Britain Can Make It in countless ways.

The generation of freelance poster and graphic designers who had shown their skills during the War also moved into the post-War period with few difficulties. The prevailing atmosphere of optimism and social utopianism that characterised post-War Britain sustained their commitment to working for public campaigns and organisations: in the few years following the War, Games, for instance, had designed posters for the Post Office, BEA, the Metropolitan Police, Cancer and Polio Appeals, and The British Industries Fair. It wasn't until 1949 that commercial work, such as his posters for the *Financial Times*, Trumans Beer, Osram Lamps, the BOAC and, a little later, Guinness and *The Times* began to dominate his work-load. The idealism of men like Games, who sought to use their skills to inform and teach rather than to sell, exactly matched the mood of post-War Britain. In contrast, he is now critical of the results of that youthful optimism, maintaining that it was 'A utopian dream that fell flat on its face'. His sense of deep disillusion stems from a feeling that the idealism was based on naivety and that it could only be born of a period of hardship, not one of plenty.

However naive it may seem in retrospect, the idealism of the post-War years generated, in the area of British graphics, an outstanding body of work. A combination of the strongly individual designs and the fiery enthusiasm that created them resulted in a British graphic design movement which lasted well through the 1950s — until the time, in fact, when American advertising agencies became increasingly influential. This movement manifested itself in posters, typography, book covers and other printed material. It was characterised by a communicative conciseness combined with a creative use of surrealistic motifs and technqiues: it was visible both at Britain Can Make It and at the Festival of Britain of 1951 and became known internationally as the British style. Within this movement Abram Games played an important role. In addition to posters he also worked on book covers. In 1944 he designed a series of twelve covers for the Pilot Press, called *Targets for Tomorrow*. For Penguin, he art directed their first set of full colour picture covers, now collectors' items.

*'Your Talk May K
Your Comrades',
1942*

Financial Times poster, 1958

'Serve As a Soldier, Vote As a Citizen', 1944

55

It was an immensely active period during which Games even had a go at product design. The commission came from a longstanding friend who owned the Cona coffee machine company. The brief was to design a new coffee-making machine to replace the old, Victorian piece of equipment which had been on the market for decades. Inevitably, as in so many other post-War products, the key material was aluminium (so much scrap was available from wartime production) and Games evolved a highly sculptural design which meant that he had to become intimately acquainted with the details of metal moulding and casting techniques. It was an exercise demonstrating, for Games, that the design process was so fundamental that it could be applied to practically any artefact, whether in two or three dimensions.

Games has retained a fascination for product design but is adamant that it is a different process from 'styling' which so often passes for product design. For him it means going back to the beginning and, if a machine is involved, disassembling it and starting from scratch. It was a philosophy which created problems for him when, in the 1950s, at the request of Sigmund Gestetner, he worked on the redesign of that company's duplicating machine. Unlike Raymond Loewy, whose design job for Gestetner over 20 years earlier had involved the application of a body-shell to conceal the mechanism, Games took the machine completely apart in his studio and redesigned not only the components but its entire mechanism. With Gestetner's death, he lost his support for the project and the design was never implemented. Disappointed but undaunted he set about inventing and designing his own 'photo-copier'. With no scientific background this proved a long haul demanding absolute faith in his abilities to learn what was needed as he went along. The result was a prototype which delivered plain paper copies at very fast rates. After many setbacks Unilever and IBM each took long options on a licence and Games felt his faith fully justified. Both options expired without licences being taken up however; the newer work and rights for electrostatic systems were just becoming available and Games' process probably offered a narrower market. An IBM scientist remarked that Games shared the 'bee syndrome': the bee was the wrong shape, too heavy, its wings were too small for it to fly but the bee didn't know all that so it flew. Games' process, according to best scientific assessment, was also impossible . . . but it worked — and rather well too.

While the practice of product design emerged naturally from Games' concerns in the 1940s and 1950s it was only ever undertaken for friends or for himself when a challenge arose which could not go unmet. He remained, professionally, primarily a graphic artist, still working independently from home as he had in the 1930s, more like a solitary designer–inventor than a member of a consultant design office seeking to make links with manufacturing industry on a highly commercial basis. He regrets the alliance that occurred between poster designers and the

The Cona Rex Coffee machine, 1951
(Photography by Stefan Bajic)

commercial world in the 1950s and maintains that, 'when posters were switched entirely to commercial purposes the general trend was a lowering of the standard once more, with the advertiser dictating the terms on which he wanted posters and the designer having to conform or he did not get his commission.' He also bemoans the demise of chromo-lithography and the impact of photo-lithography and colour photography, developments which he feels have had detrimental effects on the poster. With photo-lithography, for instance, he comments, 'The poster is de-personalised, it goes up in front of the camera and the camera does the separations and everything else.' Equally he maintains that the post-War advertising agencies, which got going again in the

1950s, did not 'employ individual artists to anything like the extent that they were used before the war or during the war.' Games explained that they were ousted in favour of teams of 'copywriters, art directors, motivational researchers, salesmen, and psychologists' which accelerated the end of individualism in poster design. In spite of such comments, Games is by no means a technological reactionary and welcomes the opportunities offered today by computer graphics. Acknowledging that the poster as he knew it has outlived its usefulness (commercial television saw to that) he is excited by the new possibilities offered by lasers, holograms and photocopying.

Of all his projects executed in the 1940s and 50s, Games is undoubtedly best known for his emblem for the Festival of Britain (see page 55). Designed initially in 1948 it underwent a number of modifications before it reached its final form. The severity of the first submission was softened, for instance, by the addition of an array of flags which Games calls the 'washing line'. It became a familiar appendage of the popular landscape in the early 1950s as it featured on so many of the Festival souvenirs from ties to horse-brasses. Games comments himself on its importance to his career, 'I suppose the emblem itself became a landmark in my own professional career as it was so well known — people identified me with it, and as a consequence 1951 itself became a key year for me and I did more posters during 1951 and 52 I suppose than at any other time.'

Games' total output of published posters numbers about 285 and it is with that particular medium that his name is lastingly associated. With the decline of the hand-drawn personalised poster as an information and advertising tool, he has moved into the background to some extent but has remained active right up the present day, allying himself with various causes and sustaining his commitment to the use of posters to speak about fundamentals not products. It is a difficult and demanding self-imposed task but one which he has fulfilled absolutely. He writes 'I'm a designer who has always worked entirely alone in graphic design. I enjoy the craftsmanship, I like to make my own mistakes.'

In terms of the evolution of the design profession in post-War Britain, Games personifies the creative individual craftsman who applied his skills to mass production in a period before American commercialism dictated the way that that job should be done. From the mid-1950s onwards the professional graphic design team moved into a different direction from the one that Games and others like him had established during and just after the War, and the large design offices which dominate the British design and advertising profession today are committed to the commercial ethic rather than to mass education: they work in the service of the 'corporation' rather than the human being. Abram Games represents the end of a British design tradition which, beginning with William Morris, combined artistic individualism with social concern. It is a tradition which still has something to say to us.

THE INDUSTRIAL DESIGNER IN BRITAIN 1946–82
Wally Olins

Two minority, slightly 'loopy' interests of the immediate post-War generation have become fashionable, commercially successful, mainstream businesses in the 1980s. They are health food and design. Who would have thought in the 1940s that there might come a time when fish and chips was threatened by bean salad? For that matter who could have envisaged that the major issue in a takeover battle between two retailing giants would largely depend on which is the better at using design.

Nobody in 1946 could conceivably have predicted the overwhelming success of the design business 40 years later. There was no precedent for it. And it didn't happen overnight. Although Britain Can Make It was a revelation to a visually starved public — it seemed to be about a Utopian world — I cannot think that it made any real lasting impact in a popular sense.

In the 40s, it was almost axiomatic that Good Design could not be popular; it could only be forced on a reluctant mass audience which, given the slightest opportunity, would choose meretricious rubbish instead. The Labour Government of the late 40s was sternly paternalistic. It supported the Ground Nuts Scheme, nationalisation, Freedom for India, Export and as part of this mixed dollop of medicine — in a half-hearted kind of way — it also supported Good Design.

Through the 50s, design remained related to middle-class good taste, with what we might today call 'Radical Chic'. In so far as people talked about design, which wasn't much outside the Council of Industrial Design, discussion centred around the idea of whether Good Design — by which was meant award-winning design, could ever sell anything. This was not a climate in which design could easily flourish.

There were a few leading designers who had established a reputation for themselves by the post-War period. Some of them like Ashley Havinden and Milner Gray had emerged from the British tradition, all Arts and Crafts, quirky humour, tweeds and pipes; the others, represented by Henrion and Hans Schleger, had come from Europe. They brought with them the sterner, austere, more rigorous traditions associated with the Bauhaus. These designers had what were by today's standards small businesses; then they were called practices. Most only employed two or three assistants: a practice with more than ten people was big. An exception to this was the Design Research Unit run by

Misha Black and Milner Gray — a comparatively large organisation. Black, of Russian origin, was an ardent and successful proselytiser for design, who sought, and usually found, patrons amongst big businesses.

Clients were usually big companies, or sometimes their advertising agencies, who needed, as they might have put it, 'something in the way of design'. Exhibition stands were a staple; so was packaging. Some of the breweries used designers for beer labels. In addition to the larger companies, some smaller specialised manufacturing companies, like Hille and Ernest Race in furniture, also employed designers for their enthusiast marketplaces.

By the middle 50s, design had become a sizeable cottage industry. In London there were hundreds of designers, working at this time for large companies or advertising agencies, or for the Central Office of Information. The government was a major design patron in the areas of products, exhibitions, graphics and interiors.

The designer had a rather uncomfortable and equivocal position in the commercial world. Many designers thought of themselves as professional people, like architects or doctors. They devised inhibiting, restrictive practices: for many years, for instance, the professional code forbade advertising, 'cold calling' on potential clients and competition on price. Naturally they charged in guineas. In a nutshell design was quaint, somewhat precious and only of peripheral significance to the real world.

For most industrial companies, however, design hardly existed. While few of the larger British companies employed 'stylists' or designers, most designers, even those who were comparatively well known, lived on a jobbing basis, in a close and rather uncomfortable relationship with the advertising agency. The advertising agency did everything: it produced ads, designed packs and exhibition stands, advised on store layout and so on. The 50s was the heyday of the big one-stop-shopping advertising agency. Clients tended to rely on their advertising agency for all kinds of creative and marketing services, way beyond advertising. One or two agencies even had their own supermarkets to test clients' packaging and point-of-sale material. In the clients' mind the major agencies may not always have produced Good Design but by God they were commercial. So while Good Design might be all right to use when it didn't really matter, when there was something commercially important involved, they felt that it was probably better to stick with the agency. After all, the advertising agency was deemed to be the place where creative ideas were success-fully married to business.

There were important exceptions to the rule, of course. Even in the 50s, and certainly in the early 60s, a few of Britain's major enterprises used designers on a massive scale. Dr Beeching's British Railways under the leadership of George Williams, perhaps one of the earliest design

No.1 in Europe

managers, appointed the DRU to work on what must be one of the largest identity schemes ever to be commissioned in the UK. Henrion, at about the same time, was carrying out identity programmes not only for BEA, one of the forerunners of British Airways, but also for KLM in Holland.

The breakthrough began in the early 60s. But the change in pace was barely perceptible to those of us involved at the time. It is much easier to see what happened in retrospect. Many of today's design consultancy leaders moved into design in the late 50s and early 60s. David Ogle and Tom Karen, for instance, formed Ogle Design in the early 50s; James Pilditch started his Allied International Designers in the late 50s; Fletcher, Forbes and Gill (the forerunner of Pentagram) emerged in about 1962–3, and Wolff Olins came on the scene in 1964–5. At about that time too, Terence Conran, sick of trying to peddle furniture that no retailer wanted to sell, set up his first Habitat shop in the Fulham Road.

In retrospect it seems clear that this new generation of designers was dramatically different from most of its predecessors. They were aggressive commercially and less inhibited by a quasi-professional stance. Many of the designers knew, liked and even socialised with advertising people. The atmosphere of the time was different too. People keep telling me that the 60s was some kind of golden age for British design and designers. For those of us working in small, struggling, financially fragile businesses, it didn't feel like it at the time.

There is no doubt though that the creative climate definitely changed, and the emergence of pop music, the Beatles, mini-skirts and other mass cultural influences deriving from these 60s phenomena gave inspiration to the young design companies struggling to make it. It affected clients too. More people inside companies began to look at design in a more inquiring and open-minded fashion. Design became less formal,

61

less a minority taste, in a real sense less an arcane series of products for a small, highly educated self-selecting audience. For the first time design in Britain started to become accessible — even popular. As it became accessible and popular, it also started to become commercial. The commercial instincts of the new young design companies combined with the lively original work which they produced expanded the market.

The cloistered, rarified and somewhat genteel world of design was shattered. The new designers got a great deal of help from much the most influential design spokesman of the day, Paul Reilly — later Lord Reilly. Practically single handed he spent the 1960s making design respectable. Although he was of an older generation and part of a tradition which found the new design thinking shocking, he saw that it had a vigour and vitality, and an ability to touch and influence ordinary people, which had, for the most part, previously been lacking in the design world. And Reilly pushed design.

One of the big design victories with which Reilly was personally associated was the new QE2. The Cunard company's senior executives were persuaded, after a public, acrimonious debate, to appoint professional designers to look after what they called 'decor' — a preserve previously allocated to their wives and daughters.

During the 60s, many British designers exploited, and were exploited by, a massive wave of creativity. Paul Reilly's Design Council was also active in promoting the cause of British design abroad. Reilly's efforts received backing from an unlikely source, a new organisation, the D&AD — Designers and Art Directors Association — formed by an ex ad-man, Edward Booth-Clibborn, partly, at any rate, to bridge the gap between designers and art directors and also to take up the design export challenge. And that's how export began. Somewhat to their surprise British design and British designers actually became fashionable internationally.

In all the major European countries with a great design tradition — Italy with its architect–product designer base; Germany with the Bauhaus–Ulm tradition; Scandinavia with its respect for simplicity and natural materials — designers continued in the 60s to design and carry out their business activities in much the same way as they always had. The revolution that was taking place in the UK design world simply passed them by. Typically, on the Continent, there were small studios led by a respected master surrounded by a few acolytes. The work which they produced was of a very high standard and, although much of it was highly praised and heavily publicised, it remained a minority taste, in which relatively few manufacturers were involved.

In the US things had been different for a long time. The days of the great industrial design era of the 30s and 40s were ending: Henry Dreyfuss, Walter Dorwin Teague and the others were winding down, but in their place other kinds of companies were emerging.

Apart from a few grandees like Eliot Noyes and Saul Bass, who worked with small groups, the Americans were tough, aggressive and comparatively big. Firms like Loewy/Snaith and Lippincott and Margulies employed between 50 and 100 people. A few employed even more. They attempted with some success to work for clients across a wide range of activities, largely based around the visual identity of the whole corporation. But they also worked on store design, packaging, what they called exhibits — anything in fact they could lay their hands on. Their design work was to our European eyes stereotyped and perhaps a bit crass, but it was certainly noticeable. The great thing about American design companies was that they shared a common vocabulary with businessmen. They talked about marketing and share price and profit. Their work was not an inspiration to the new British design companies, but their attitudes were.

The British designers actually saw that companies, tough commercial companies — not just patrons but industrialists and businessmen who had no emotional commitment to design — were prepared to pay big money to designers because they thought design worked commercially. They thought that design would help their companies to be more visible — or that it would help them to sell more products. British designers began to realise that they had flair and wit, that their work was easy to understand, that they had the discipline of the Europeans and the commercial instincts of the Americans, and that's when, for the first time since the great days at the turn of the century, British designers began to export.

During the early 70s, for example, Wolff Olins was carrying out massive corporate identity programmes for Renault and VW/Audi world-wide. It is perhaps symptomatic of the state of British design and its relationship with British industry at that time that we couldn't even get British Leyland to bother to come and see what we were doing for their much more successful competitors. Nor were the press in this country much help: they trivialised and distorted design. Or as we tended to put it at the time, they put design on the women's page. So it wasn't easy.

As the 70s wore on the new design consultancies grew bigger — they won more than they lost though. In the early 70s, 20 people was a big design firm; by the mid-70s, a few of the larger British companies employed as many as 50 people, and 20 had become quite commonplace. It was at this time that the multi-disciplinary consultancy began to emerge in Britain. Pentagram was one of the first to introduce this pattern. The original Pentagram team was formed from young, well known, highly successful graphic designers. In a move which seemed revolutionary at the time, they were joined a few years later by architects (Theo Crosby) and product designers (Kenneth Grange) so that they could offer a complete design package. Other British design consultancies — they no longer called themselves practices, but hadn't quite got around to calling themselves companies — were startled by this Pentagram move and began to emulate it.

Success starts to breed success. As design was beginning to show signs of growth, so in the early 70s another crop of design companies, largely spawned from the first generation of aggressive companies, began to emerge. These were more hard nosed and tougher than their predecessors. Rodney Fitch, who had worked for Terence Conran, started up on his own. He concentrated mostly on retail design, and within a very short time he became astonishingly and very publicly successful, catching up and overtaking companies ten years older than his own.

Although design in packaging, new product development, products, interiors, and in the whole concept which we call corporate identity made rapid progress in terms of recognition as an industrial tool, the really big breakthrough came in the retail business. Traditionally, mainstream retailers had ignored design. With a few exceptions (mostly fringe experimenters or specialists) they had used it neither in relation to their products nor their environments. Almost single-handed Terence Conran reversed this trend and, during the 60s and 70s, forced the retail world to accept the power of design as a commercial resource. It is perhaps a little early to get Conran's achievement into perspective, but there can be no doubt that, virtually alone, he demonstrated that good design can be popular, accessible and above all commercially viable.

Retail design exploded, and a few designers and design companies saw this opportunity and rushed in. Those companies that were able to adapt themselves to the demands of their clients got big contracts. Big contracts led to big publicity — and to big budgets — and this in turn led to design companies adopting a more professional approach.

Packaging design by Michael Peters & Partners, 1973

Again in turn, this meant that they were taken more seriously by the press and by potential clients. A virtuous circle had been started.

Since the big breakthrough days of the mid 70s, the process has continued. We seem to have reached a critical mass in which design, because it seems significant both commercially and culturally, is becoming accepted as an integral part of the British scene. And all this is very new. In business, design is starting (but only starting) to emerge as a standard, normal resource of equal significance with finance, advertising, research & development and so on.

As a matter of course designers are employed across a wide range of industries. In the retailing world the 1985 Debenhams/Burton takeover battle was fought largely over design issues — a situation impossible to conceive even as recently as 1980. In new product development — almost a new discipline — graphic and product designers work with researchers and marketing people of various kinds to develop and produce new products. Identity is now perceived by some companies as a corporate resource of immense value. Identity design is perceived only to be truly effective when it is linked with a communications programme, which forces design companies to work increasingly with public relations, advertising and personnel people as one group. Increasingly too, identity design is seen as the visible manifestation of corporate strategy.

The cause of design has been seriously and vigorously taken up by government. At the time of writing, John Butcher is the Under-Secretary at the Department of Trade and Industry charged with responsibility for propagating the value and power of design. This must be the first time that any British government has taken proper notice of design since Prince Albert's day. He even has a budget for promoting design. A few years ago all this was quite inconceivable.

Interior for 'Next' in Slough by Conran Associates

The Unlisted Securities Market has made some designers rich. A few have become paper millionaires. Much more important it has forced the City and financial journalists to take a look at the design business, and attempt to assess it as a growth stock. However hazy, confused and ill-informed the City is — muddling up design companies with advertising agencies and public relations companies — it is now at last aware that design exists, that it is serious, that it has commercial significance. The first design consultancy to go for a public quote was James Pilditch's Aidcom. He was quickly followed by Fitch, Peters and then a few others.

The experience of public scrutiny, of being publicly accountable, is very stressful. It drives companies to become more efficient, less self indulgent and more commercially aggressive. It raises the real issue of whether all this actually improves design standards and is good for the business in the longer term.

Now that the power of design is emerging as a recognisable force, attention is beginning to turn (both within the design business and outside it), to how design should be managed as a resource. Until now most designers and clients saw design as a one-off jobbing activity; now that it is emerging as a management resource we have to learn how to use it as part of a corporate system.

At the London Business School Peter Gorb has set up one of the world's first design management units. Here business school students learn as part of their curriculum what design is and how it has to be managed in business. Gorb's initiative is being emulated elsewhere in Britain and followed closely in the US and Europe. All in all design in Britain has never been so influential. It was inconceivable, even to the most optimistic of us who went into design in the early 60s, that it should have come so far so fast. And the pace of development is increasing.

But all of this success needs qualification. First, we have to have a sense of proportion. Although in some industries like drink, transport, retailing and, increasingly, financial services, design has made a big mark, in most it has not even made so much as a scratch. Much of British industry remains as ignorant of the power of design resource as it ever was.

Second, the strain on British designers to grow and to adapt to their new opportunities has created stress within the design world. The small, quiet, cottage industry world where like-minded enlightened craftsmen could share their minority interests has practically disappeared, at least in the major urban centres. Even the antipathy, the traditional hostility which existed between designer and industry has become, or is becoming, irrelevant. Terence Conran and others have shown that good design *can* mean good business. But a lot of designers are unprepared for this and don't like it. They feel that their creativity is somehow threatened. They want to be left alone to produce 'good design'.

But what is 'good design'? Is it simply commercially successful design? Some of the very large companies in the design business maintain traditional quality standards. In graphics particularly, but in product and fashion design too, British design has never had a higher reputation internationally.

On the other hand a few of the bigger companies, and quite a lot of the smaller ones too, find themselves unable to resist the pressure to bash the stuff out. With so much more design work being produced than ever before, some of it is bound to suffer. And all this is naturally creating distress within the profession. If you can still call it a profession.

On the whole though, British design and British designers have never been so successful, never been so sought after, never had such high standards and never been so rich. What more could anybody reasonably ask? Well, the answer to that is quite a lot. Over the next few years Britain has a very good chance of developing what could become a significant design industry in world terms. But the precise place of such an industry remains unclear. Is design really part of the marketing process? Is design the visual manifestation of a communications policy, or a corporate strategy? Is design intended solely to differentiate the product, so that the manufacturer can charge more for it? Does design have an educational mission? Will computer-aided design change the shape and nature of the design industry? Will design companies continue to expand so that staff of 200–300 become quite commonplace? Is design becoming a major part of the international information technology business? Nobody really knows.

Only one thing is certain, British designers live in stirring times. Things have never been more exciting.

Part 4

Design and British Industry

The focus of this part is the highly problematic but supremely relevant question of the relationship of design with British manufacturing in the period since 1946. The first two chapters concentrate on textiles — selected because it is a traditional, craft-based industry — and examine both the changes in that industry since 1946 and the role that design has played in these changes. Mary Schoeser, a writer, historian and archivist at Warners Fabrics, provides a succinct overview of the area, while Eddie Pond, a textile and wallpaper designer who has been involved with the British textiles industry since the 1950s, offers a more subjective account of the same area.

The second set of essays focuses on product manufacturing and design. The first is an interview between Kenneth Grange of the Pentagram Design group (and probably the best known and most highly respected product designer in this country) and his personal assistant, Mary Alexander, which constitutes another personal view of the relationship between British manufacturing industry and design in the last few decades. The second is a case study, written by myself, of the way that Thorn EMI, the largest producer of consumer electronics — the other end of the manufacturing spectrum — in this country at the moment, has defined and used design since 1946.

This part looks closely at both the strengths and weaknesses of the particular way in which British manufacturing industry uses design. In so doing, it attempts to show where lessons for the future might be learned.

'GOOD DESIGN AND GOOD BUSINESS':

A SURVEY OF THE CHANGES IN THE BRITISH TEXTILE INDUSTRY 1946–86

MARY SCHOESER

It is said that Lord Gowrie once described textile manufacture as the UK's most inquired-into industry. This is hardly surprising. At one point in the 19th century Lancashire looms produced half of all that UK manufacturers exported; today only 2% of those looms are still working. Clearly something dramatic has happened, and most of it has happened in the past 40 years. Thus any assessment of the changes within the textile industry since the end of the Second World War must be either lengthy or selective. What follows is a generalised survey of the major trends since 1946, for which, *in every case*, there are exceptions. Further, the statistics presented should not be taken only in their most obvious sense. The collapse of the Lancashire industry, for example, certainly sent shock waves through the industry in the 1950s. In the longer term, however, there were benefits in breaking the mould of traditional attitudes to large-volume production. The 'big is beautiful' thinking (which persisted into the 1960s) meant standardisation. It required 'safe' markets, capable of absorbing large amounts of cloth while making few demands for changes in design. In retrospect it is clear that these markets were disappearing or being taken over by production from developing countries. It is equally clear that design (both technical and 'visual') was to play a much greater part in the new industry which evolved, albeit slowly, in subsequent years.

Against this background Britain Can Make It was significant as being the first exhibition to take as a principle 'the excellence of British design and designers'[1] (as opposed to manufacturers) and to explain to the uninitiated just what 'design' meant. The setting up of the exhibition was one of the first acts of the Council of Industrial Design, whose Chairman was Sir Thomas Barlow, a baron of the Lancashire textile industry. His own firm, Barlow & Jones, had spawned Helios as an offshoot in the 1930s: this was one of the first companies to provide *reasonably priced*, well designed furnishing fabrics to the retail trade.[2] The CoID's promotional catch-phrase for Britain Can Make It was 'Good Design — and Good Business', and the exhibition set out to encourage manufacturers to produce well designed products at a time when shortages meant that even the most badly designed product would sell. To what extent the exhibition was immediately successful is difficult to assess, but it is possible to trace the gradual acceptance of its philosophy by focusing on the way in which events influenced the role of the designer over the following 40 years. In doing so no attempt has been made to chronicle that which was expected to change — namely style.

The increasingly frequent and diverse textile 'fashion' developments that characterise the past 40 years have their roots in the social and economic upheaval of the 1920s and 30s. In 1932 Wells Coates redecorated a London flat, untouched since 1893. The original interiors — ornate, ostentatious and over-crowded — ' . . . displayed an absolute certainty of the permanence of social conditions which we now know were extremely impermanent . . . Nobody conscious of existing conditions would be mad enough to try, even if he were fool enough to want, to carry on such a tradition.'[3]

This comment was particularly apt on its re-publication in 1944. Photographs comparing interiors from 1946 and 1986 do not show such radical alteration as that seen in Wells Coates' example, although some has certainly occurred. Tastes have changed, but they are still influenced by the 'extremely impermanent' conditions to which the author, Miller, referred. To take but one example, much that was shown at Britain Can Make It was emphasized as being suitable for small rooms. Although the arrangement and appearance of furniture within rooms has altered since 1946, the disposition of the textiles used has remained more or less constant. The scale of rooms has not since radically altered either, but increased spending power among the younger section of the population, particularly from the late 1950s to early 70s, has meant both an earlier entry into the housing market (buying *and* renting) and more frequent changes in residence, and therefore furnishings. More

Dining room and living room before and after alteration by Wells Coates in 1932 (Courtesy of Studio Publications)

72

clothing was bought too, so that world-wide consumption of fibres per person is now over five times greater than it was in 1946. There should have been a parallel increase in the opportunities for the UK's manufacturers but this has not been the case. By the early 1970s Britain was using more imported than home-produced fabric.[4]

To understand the changed role of design within the textile industry over the past 40 years, one must first look at the conditions within some of the manufacturing sections which directed attention away from the need to make greater and more appropriate use of designers. It is essential to stress here how varied are the components which make up the industry: polymer chemists, machine builders, yarn spinners, bleachers, dyers and garment makers are all intimately tied to those processes generally regarded as textile production — that is, weaving and printing. The shift in the relative importance of these elements has had considerable influence on designers. In 1946 the industry could broadly be broken up into the consumer products (woven and printed apparel and furnishing fabrics) and woven household textiles and carpets. It is only since then that knitted, tufted, and non-woven textiles have been mass produced. Industrial textiles made their way into tyres, tennis balls, artificial turf and beyond, into a wide range of engineering and production technologies. In 1946 hardly anyone could have foreseen an aramid fibre (such as Du Pont's 'Kevlar') with five times the strength of steel. Such developments relied largely on synthetic fibres, the first of which was nylon, introduced in 1939.[5] In industrial applications 'performance is everything and aesthetics count for very little.'[6] However, with just over 15% of production in the EEC concentrated in this area, the majority of textiles still require attention to design and colour. Within traditional areas of textile production there have been varying degrees of innovation and relative growth or decline over the past 40 years, but there is little doubt that the two most significant factors overall are the introduction of new fibres together with the widespread restructuring of the industry as a whole. The synthetics 'boom' began in the UK in 1951, when Courtaulds set up the world's largest processing plant. A 20 year period of rapid expansion followed, during which time many other firms were acquired by the growing textile giants who controlled a large manufacturing force from a small, centralised management — and prospered. Early in the 1970s, however, the recession combined with extensive over-capacity to bring this growth to a dramatic halt. ICI alone, in its consequent restructuring, shed over 60% of its synthetic fibres labour force in Western Europe. Up to that point the major changes in machinery had concentrated on the improvement of known techniques — largely resulting in higher speed and higher volume production. The implication for the designer was the continuation of the Lancashire legacy of standardisation. When Courtaulds took over Morton Sundour in 1963, for example, it was reported of their avant-garde subsidiary, Edinburgh Weavers, that 'the glory seems to have departed'.[7] One contemporary observer recalls the terrifying rapidity with which offices and showrooms merged or disappeared in London during this period[8] (for London had replaced Lancashire as the hub of the textile industry, being better placed for exports and for fashion imports). This is not to suggest that design was completely ignored by the textile giants. The large synthetic fibre and fabric firms must be credited with vast improvements in the ingredients and technologies which all designers had at their disposal. Hand in hand with the rapid increase in the production and development of synthetics came new and better dyes, both for natural and man-made fibres, together with the promotion of colour prediction services. In her essay on furnishing fabrics in *Design 46*, Enid Marx lamented that 'synthetic dyes tend to be harsh and brittle in colour. Though they can give great brilliance, especially on rayon, this does not make up for their lack of depth . . . Our problem is to make our colours as beautiful as they are durable.'[9] This is not a restriction faced by designers today.

As a general rule, the introduction of new yarns and processes was initially accompanied by design limitations. Synthetic yarns, for example, could not be textured until the mid 1960s. Only subsequent improvements in both the texture and handle of yarns has brought back to the designer a range of 'fancy' yarns which were ruled out for a good part of the 40 years under discussion, due to a combination of technical and economic restrictions. (To a great extent technical restrictions most affected man-made fibres and economic ones, natural yarns, particularly wool.) Some processes have only recently developed beyond their initial limitations; for example, tufting, which was introduced for the manufac-

ture of household textiles and carpets in 1953 and which is now the dominant means of carpet production in the UK, could only employ two colours until recently. The application of microcomputer-controlled patterning systems early in the 1980s made it possible to use as many colours as were traditionally found in woven Axminster carpets. (Significantly, only three or four colours *are* used, but this is a conscious design choice.) The knitting industry has also made widespread use of computerised design and production techniques, and is another sector which benefited from the support of synthetic fibre manufacturers, who saw knitted fabrics as a logical end-use for their yarns. Double jersey knitting was brought to the UK by Hungarian refugees in the mid 1950s. It too suffered when the synthetics market contracted in the early 1970s, but knit*wear* has since become the success story of the past decade, with exports matching imports. Finally, a boost to prints also came indirectly from the man-made fibres sector, with the introduction of transfer printing in the late 1960s. Development of new yarns and technologies extended the areas in which designers could work. At the same time both new methods and the increased mechanisation of known methods boosted productivity, so that today spinning speeds are eight times faster and weaving five times faster than in 1946.

Impressive as these figures may sound, they must be assessed against the background of the retraction of the industry as a whole. Increased productivity was necessary to enable the British industry to compete with low-wage, labour-intensive textile industries developing outside Europe. However, these conditions were clearly detrimental to the home work-force. In the wake of the streamlining of the man-made fibres industry came an influx of imports — aided by the strong pound at the end of the 1970s and (some would say) by the failure of British manufacturers to respond quickly to changes in fashion. These factors affected the whole of the industry. Between 1972 and 1982 employment fell by 65%; yarn and cloth production fell by 50%. For designers the most significant decline was that of the figured wovens, against which there were many factors at work. The Italians, employing British skills and technology acquired in the early 1950s, quickly took over the UK market for medium-priced woollen apparel cloths, and the combined forces of man-made fibres and knitted fabrics also cut into woven fashion fabric sales.

The worst blow, however, arose out of the collapse of the Lancashire cotton cloth industry, which also supported the bulk of the engraved roller printing in this country. It may seem contradictory that the demise of a printing industry should adversely effect wovens, but it did so by clearing the way for the rise of screen printing, which had none of the disadvantages of the printing process it replaced. Innovative design had been prohibited in roller printing due to the high cost of engraving the pattern,[10] and repeat sizes were limited by the circumference of the roller. Hand screen printing had already become a vehicle for avant-garde designs prior to the War, and a number of firms (including Tootal, Broadhurst & Lee, F W Grafton, A Walton, Ascher, Warners and Helios) submitted screen printed fashion and furnishing fabrics to Britain Can Make It. In *Design 46*, Audrey Withers, writing on fashion and dress fabrics, commented that, ' . . . though all too many (roller) prints are sadly lacking both in design and fashion qualities, yet certain enlightened firms are commissioning artists and designers of the first order to produce fabrics and scarves of real distinction.'[11] She listed Henry Moore, Graham Sutherland, Felix Topolski, Hans Tisdall, Cecil Beaton and Julian Trevelyn, all of whom produced designs for screen prints — a process which Enid Marx in the same publication described as 'adopted by our more enterprising manufacturers . . . more venture-some with new designs'. Because of them, Marx went on to predict, 'a great renaissance in England textile design, once the present shortages have been relieved.'[12] She was correct. Once screen printing became fully mechanised in the 1950s, it offered advantages of economic production and flexible design, which together meant it could respond quickly to rapid changes in fashion. It is little wonder that it prospered.[13] For virtually the whole of the 40 years since the War, screen prints are the dominant source of patterned textiles, with firms such as David Whitehead (in the 1950s and 60s) and Hull Traders and Heal Fabrics Ltd (in the 1960s and 70s) setting trends with their boldly designed fabrics.

Woven furnishing fabrics at this time were limited by escalating yarn costs, so that by the early 1970s furnishing fabrics were mainly printed cotton (and printed on fabrics not manufactured in the UK). Transfer and screen-printed polyester/cotton sheets were then increasing in sales, with an initial impact on UK dyers. However, with the rising popularity of duvets another traditional area of British wovens manufacture was affected — that of blankets and bedcovers. It is instructive to look at women's magazines and design journals of the past 40 years, in which one can see the decline of wovens and the rise of prints. It is no exaggeration to say that possibilities for wovens designers working within the industry were severely curtailed by these changes. Those that survived did so in the 'up-market' contract furnishing and high fashion areas. Thus in the now vastly diminished woollen industry, firms such as Reid & Taylor, Neill of Langholme and Holywell Textiles produce fashion fabrics which rely on high quality and market-directed design — exporting the majority of their output. Further afield, wovens designers made their mark as designer–makers or fibre artists. It cannot simply be coincidence that the major period of innovative fibre 'sculpture' occurred at the same time as the standardisation and/or decline of industrial wovens manufacture.

Another indirect contribution to design was made first by the growth of large textile consortia and later by the recession in the industry. A gap was created in the market for specialised or limited production fabrics, most often with a high design content. In this climate the designer–maker became established, producing handwoven or tufted rugs and handwoven, printed or painted fabrics, some later moving into mechanised production and taking their textiles into finished garment form, as did Laura Ashley and Zandra Rhodes.

A final word must be said regarding the importance of technical developments since 1946. The increasingly competitive market spurred man-made fibre manufacturers to improve their technology and overcome the disadvantages of early synthetics (poor draping, non-absorption, yellowing, dirt attraction). By the mid 1960s, new synthetics began to appear with advantages such as minimum-iron, easy stain release, drip dry, permanently shrunk or pleated. Soon, across the industry, standards of colour-fastness and overall quality improved to such an extent that they began to be taken for granted. The better performance and handle of cloths — particularly in the blends and finishing of various fibres — has also broken down traditional concepts of 'end-use'. In fashion, these improvements have stemmed the tide of opinion which began to turn against synthetics in the mid 1970s. Fashion buyers in the UK today consume more man-made fibres than cotton, wool, silk and linen combined, principally because it is now possible to blend fibres or combine yarns to give, for example, the performance of acrylic and nylon with the character of wool, mohair and cotton.[14] Fabrics for warmth have further been affected by increased production of cars and

'Midhurst' textile design, adapted from a mid-19th century document in 1949 by Wolfs Purger for Warner Sons

use of central heating. Thus, winter clothes and bedding, typically wool in 1946, are seldom if at all simply that today. The consumer now chooses by appearance and touch, leaving it to the manufacturer to ensure that the cloth or garment performs as it should.

The gradual abstraction of 'surface' from 'substance' (accelerated by the mechanisation of screen printing with its painterly treatment of cloth) had already begun at the end of the War, when variety was at a premium. A clear indication of this trend can be found in the Society of Industrial Artist's third volume of *Designers in Britain*, which commemorated their 21st anniversary and the Festival of Britain in 1951. In it industrial design was divided into two categories: 'form' and 'pattern'. Everything *but* textiles was included under 'form'. This separation is worth noting, for it underlines the way in which textiles were increasingly promoted: by appearance, by designer or by house-style. Indeed, the proliferation of ever more sophisticated promotional campaigns, whether editorials, advertising, trade shows or exhibitions, is a post-War characteristic.

A significant early lead into the arena of promotion was given by the Cotton Board, which established its 'Colour, Design and Style Centre' in 1940, four years before the Council of Industrial Design came into being. From its base in Manchester the Centre pushed for a higher standard of design in British cottons, employing 'startling and original'[15] exhibitions created by Jimmy Cleveland Belle, director until

1950, Donald Tomlinson, director from 1950 to 1964 and Frederick Lyle, director from 1964 to 1969. By 1962 the Centre was commemorating its 100th exhibition, among which were some (for example, on Scandinavian textiles in the mid 1940s and on English chintzes in the mid 1950s) which had had a seminal influence on textile fashions of the period. The 100th exhibition showed the work of David Cunliffe and Colleen Farr, two of the first three winners (the other was Pat Albeck) of the Centre's travel scholarships for young professional textile designers. The Cotton Board actively campaigned to break down traditional barriers, particularly in the fashion industry. Here the merchant converters (middlemen organising production by textile manufacturers and selling on to garment makers or fabric retailers) were seen to have ' . . . limited the growth of the creative design function within finishing companies and may also have deterred the emergence in the UK of independent (fashion fabric) design houses along the lines of those in Milan, Como, Lyons and Paris.'[16]

In his introduction to 'Inprint', Donald Tomlinson got straight to the point, beginning: 'It seems the British cotton industry's reputation for fashion authority could hardly be lower. . . . The reputation of British cotton furnishing, on the other hand, could hardly be higher . . .' Young British fashion designers had the attention of the world when this was written (1964), yet many of these designers used imported or specially commissioned fabrics. Thus Donald Tomlinson's aim with 'Inprint' was to bring the fabric designer in contact with

SIA exhibition of design and textiles at the Cotton Board Colour, Design and Style Centre, Manchester 1951 (Courtesy of Cotton Board Manchester)

the fabric manufacturer and fashion designer, providing better, closer communications which in turn meant more immediate response to fashion changes. His campaign was the first to demonstrate the potential of consumer-oriented manufacture. Subsequent events, particularly the increasingly competitive market from the early 1970s, proved the value of direct links between fashion and fabric designers. Today it is not uncommon to find high-street fashion retail firms, such as Next or Marks & Spencer, working directly with textile designers.

It is interesting to look back to Britain Can Make It, in which the majority of printed dress fabrics were shown as lengths or, at best, scarves. The dresses themselves were largely of woven cloth. Although economic factors favoured prints and reduced the use of wovens (never displaced in fashion to the same extent as in furnishings), the Cotton Board's promotions accelerated the acceptance of printed fashion fabrics. While not necessarily all cotton, fashions of the past 30 years have largely used prints for their major surface design statement. It is only in the past five years that figured wovens have rejoined the fashion fabric vocabulary of plain, dyed and colour/weave effect cloths (stripes, checks, twills, etc). More young designers are specialising in cloth weaving today than ten years ago, perhaps due to the promise of greater

'Inprint, Infact', exhibition of 1965 at the Colour, Design and Style Centre in Manchester (Courtesy of Cotton Board Manchester)

design freedom with the application of computer-controlled patterning, as has already been demonstrated in the knitwear industry.

That there have been so many young designers ready to provide new design ideas is the result of the expansion of design education since the War. In the 1950s and 60s, however, textile design was dominated by the established art colleges: the Central School and the Royal College of Art. For example, the latter provided 12 of the 16 designers featured in the 'Inprint' exhibition already referred to, among them Pat Albeck, Colleen Farr, Audrey Levy, Althea McNish, Barbara Brown, Natalie Gibson, Howard Carter and Peter McCulloch. The designs which they and others produced in the mid 1960s were to have considerable impact through the ranges of Heal Fabrics, Liberty, F W Grafton, Tootals, Cavendish Textiles, Hull Traders, Bernard Wardle and David Whitehead, to name but a few. The design direction from within the firm was crucial to the widespread commissioning of designs. Tom Worthington at Heals, Shirley Craven at Hull Traders, Eddie Pond at Wardles and Colleen Farr at Liberty helped to establish many young designers, too numerous to enumerate here. However one cannot pass over the subject of Central School textile graduates without mention of their most well known, Terence Conran. What one journalist was led to remark about the RCA students was just as true for others, and typical of the times: 'Many of us may get a bit sick of the endless talk of the RCA young designers, some of whom do seem to market themselves more expertly than their wares, but in this instance I think the combination of a long established firm . . . and an intensely contemporary talent . . . is interesting, not just academically, but actually.'[17]

The importance of the young textile designers entering the industry in the 1950s and 60s was that they could identify with the consumer, who was often also young. Designer–makers (increasingly evident in the late 1960s and 70s) were even more closely aligned with their customers. Whether they set up on their own or sold their designs to industry, the influx of young designers brought a welcome variety of style and, more important still, a new approach to their work. Unschooled in the traditional methods of in-house training, these designers manufactured and sold on a 'learn-as-you-go' basis, making them receptive to new ideas like focus retailing, marketing and branded house styles.

As early as 1945 market research had indicated that the UK export market (by which market strength was measured) would be reduced to high quality, well designed textiles, focused at specific markets. The gradual change from a sellers' market in 1946 to a buyers' market today has confirmed this view and has made both design and marketing more important. This is reflected in the increased concentration on styling and co-ordination, the latter first exploited in the UK by Sandersons in 1962. Although first applied to their 'Triad' wallpaper and fabric range, the idea rapidly spread to fashion ranges and later to virtually every household product. A natural corollary of style consciousness was the development of retail furnishing fabric shops such as Osborne & Little, Designers Guild and Laura Ashley. Such firms joined decorators, swollen in numbers since the War, as arbiters of taste. Sandersons themselves, wholesalers from their formation in 1860, entered the retail market in 1975. It was clear that the consumer wanted 'self-service' decorating and fashion planning, as evidenced by the popularity of the many consumer-aid publications. Design services, now also a feature of today's fashion and furnishing fabric industry, range from an individual manufacturer's 'design story' to wider-based promotions by, for example, the International Wool Secretariat. As was the case prior to the War, a handful of firms continue to support avant-garde designs through the sales of their traditional lines.* Increased interest in period restoration and the desire for more traditional, albeit eclectic, interiors has gradually increased the popularity of branded house styles based on 18th and 19th century designs. Thus what Pevsner noted in 1937 about the British upper classes may well have even wider relevance today: 'Owing to general conservatism, to inborn reserve and a distrust of anything that looks strikingly new, the majority of the British upper classes still prefer period decoration.'[18] Some observers see the re-emergence of such national styles as a sign of recovery within the industry, with Western countries marketing their traditional designs side by side with the relatively international modern style — and marketing it with equal confidence.

The modern marketplace is attuned to design, yet the vast majority of young designers still aim to set up their own businesses — with the possible exception of knitwear designers, whose industry is identified by its peers as the leading sector. To what extent other areas of textile manufacture make use of British designers is still the subject of debate. It is said that many of the best designers, particularly of fashion fabrics, find work more readily in Europe. There is little comfort for UK fashion fabric manufacturers in the high volume of imported cloth taken up by our garment manufacturers, and it is equally ironic that some of these fabrics must have been designed elsewhere by British designers. Better links between art and industry have long been a British talking-point, but only in the last five years have government-funded and other agencies focused their attention on the need to bring design and design education closer to manufacture. Although the 'Colour, Design and Style Centre' is now closed,[19] its methods still have wide currency. *House & Gardens*, for example, has recently re-introduced a more broadly based version of the design award it originally offered with the backing of the Cotton Board. Its aim — as with the Crafts Council's

---

* Many of the latter are drawn from archives amassed through decades of expansion and treasured now, with so many of those acquired firms' identities gone. Within London–based firms alone, the archives of G P & J Baker, Courtaulds, Sandersons and Warners are of note.

'Texstyles' exhibition in 1984 and the Design Council's sponsorship of short-term design consultancies within manufacturing units — is to bring designers and manufacturers together. Reports and conferences on the textile industry emphasise the need for 'marketing-led' design, while educational bodies stress the need for courses on design management and industrial practice for student designers. The Textile Institute, the major international forum for technical information since 1910, began in the early 1980s to organise projects and conferences on the importance of good design and marketing to the health of the industry. In 1984 their Weaving Group provided cloth for the fashion course at Liverpool Polytechnic and showed the results at its conference in the same year. Many other examples could be cited. Much that is done today demonstrates the final acceptance of the principle put forward at Britain Can Make It. Further, 40 years later, the textile industry, having weathered enormous technical and economic changes, seems confident of its ability to act upon the wisdom of the phrase coined by the organisers of the 1946 exhibition. As John Butcher MP, Parliamentary Under-Secretary of State for Industry, said in a 1984 BTEC report: 'The importance of design to British industry and to the economy has never been greater than it is today. The struggle for supremacy in world markets and the increasing demands of the design-conscious consumer make it imperative that design is given a new prominence by industry.'

Good design, in other words, means good business.

 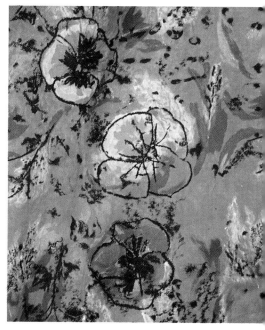

'Chelsea' and 'Belladonna', two designs by Althea McNish for Liberty of London (courtesy of John F Weiss)

ACKNOWLEDGEMENTS

I would like to thank Colleen Farr, Malcolm Burnip, Donald Tomlinson and the staff of Warner & Sons Limited for their assistance.

REFERENCES AND NOTES

1. Cripps, Sir Stafford 'Britain Can Make It' catalogue, HMSO 1946, p 1.
2. Most other avant-garde furnishing fabric firms were producing cloth for specialised projects or, if retail, at a fairly high price.
3. Miller, Duncan *Interior Decoration*: The Studio Publications, 2nd edition, 1944, p 70.
4. The statistics quoted are derived from the following sources: Burnip, Malcolm 'Changing Trends in Textile Consumption in the World', report to the Southern India Mills Association Golden Jubilee Conference, 1983; Cotton and Allied Textiles EDC *The cotton and allied textiles industry* and *Structure and prospects of the finishing sector*: NEDO 1983; 'Quarterly Stastical Review': The Textile Statistics Bureau, nos 152–7 (1984–85).
5. Rayon, a man-made cellulose-based fibre, was already available. At Britain Can Make It furnishing and fashion fabrics included rayon, but not nylon. Marks & Spencers were one of the first high-street firms to sell nylon blouses, early in the 1950s.
6. Goodall, William 'Fabrics Engineered for High Performance' p 29, in Sondhelm, W & Denyer, R (eds.) *75th Anniversary Souvenir*: The Textile Institute, 1985.
7. Design Research Unit in-house *Bulletin*, October 1966.
8. Donald Tomlinson, July 1985.
9. Marx, Enid in *Design 46: a survey of British industrial design as displayed in the 'Britain Can Make It' exhibition*: HMSO, 1946, pp 87–8.
10. Block printing was the standard method of production for high-quality furnishing fabrics prior to the War. It was expensive due to high labour and preparation costs.
11. Withers, Audrey in *Design 46*: op cit, p 46.
12. Marx, op cit, p 88.
13. Production figures for UK printed cloths rose or remained stable until 1979, while the rest of the industry was in decline from 1972.
14. There is still a strong trend in couture and high-fashion ready-to-wear for 100% natural fibre clothes. However, the example cited is taken from a Jaeger sweater, retailing in 1984 at £34.
15. Farr, Michael *Design in British Industry*, Cambridge University Press, 2nd edition, 1955, p 223.
16. *Structure and prospects of the finishing sector*: op cit, p 17.
17. Christophersen, Anita, 'The Scotsman', June 6, 1964.
18. Pevsner, Nikolaus *An Inquiry into Industrial Art in England*, Cambridge University Press, 1937, p 205.
19. See *Design 356*, 1978 for further information on the 'Colour, Design and Style Centre'.

DESIGN AND THE BRITISH TEXTILE AND WALLPAPER INDUSTRIES
EDDIE POND

Did Britain Make It? Yes, we did! The trouble was that when we came to sell it, no one really wanted it.

In the years just after 1945, Britain was virtually the only country in the world (with the exception of the USA) manufacturing quality textile products. The lack of any international competition created at that time a production-orientated complacency among UK textile manufacturers which became a main contributing factor to the demise of the industry over the following 20 years.

Britain had always been a world leader in textile products and, in the two decades after the War, we received international recognition for the innovative design quality of printed furnishing fabrics particularly. Design was recognisably split at that time into two camps — traditional and modern — a situation that does not seem to apply so much today. This meant that most producers tried a bit of both types with the end result that they did not know which camp they were supposed to be in. Neither did the customer! At a CoID seminar at the Royal Society of Arts in 1962 for designers and manufacturers, The Duke of Edinburgh opened proceedings by asking, 'What shall we talk about, traditional or modern?'

During the immediate post-War period, fortunes were made by 'allocating' fabrics, most of them having that 'Genuine Traditional Olde English Character', to the remnants of an Empire where 'the sun never set'. Whilst the design of many of these fabrics was awful, designs from companies like Sandersons, Bakers and Warners were often superb examples of their type. No UK producer, however, ever established a worthwhile market in the USA. When countries such as Australia put up tariff barriers in the early 1960s to protect their balance of payments — at just about the same time as competition arrived from Germany, France, Italy, Holland, Portugal, etc — the shock waves were to change the face of the UK textile industry for ever. Joe Hyman helped, but that's another story. Companies with great reputations such as Turnbull and Stockdale, Morton Sundour and Calico Printers Association went, and eventually Warners, Bakers, Edinburgh Weavers, Tibor Reich, Gayonnes Foxtons and many others were either sold and restructured, or disappeared without trace. Sandersons, too, was eventually sold to an American textile giant as recently as 1985.

None of this run-down could be blamed upon designers. Britain produced, and still produces, the most talented, creative and imaginative textile designers in the world (we keep telling ourselves, hoping to make it true). Whilst the statement is generally true, you will not get much agreement from Scandinavia, France, Italy or Germany. Certainly, no amount of pressure has prevented UK textile manufacturers from continuing to buy designs in Como, Milan, Paris and Lyons. Our fashion designers invariably use fashion fabrics from France and Italy. Admittedly, this situation is changing for the better, but we never came anywhere near to where the industry planned to be by now. We have never been able to create a proper atelier system in which buyers can go from one studio to another putting a collection together as they can in Como or Paris. When the Merchant Convertors Association set up their own studio in London a few years ago, it sunk without trace within a year because the members would not use it. Very few textile designers earn a living to be compared with that of leading illustrators and graphic designers. The textile designers who stick at it either sell in the USA or have a prime source of income from teaching, with one or two notable exceptions.

Many other factors have contributed to the demise of the British textile industry. The Clean Air Act, for instance, encouraged the widespread use of central heating, which in turn did away with the need for draught-excluding curtains at windows and doors. The run-down of the British furniture industry reduced the market for upholstery fabrics and, consequently, loose covers. Plastics and other synthetic fabrics lasted longer and were not replaced so often. One benefit of central heating, however, was to make the duvet nationally popular from the early 60s. This led directly to market developments in printed sheets and other bed linen, and the idea of total product co-ordination in the home, which saved many textile houses from going out of business altogether, and made others like Vantona. Co-ordination led wallpaper manufacturers into textiles, notably Coloroll, and Osborne and Little.

The market for printed dress fabrics had also declined dramatically as a result of the common acceptance of women wearing trousers, aided in the past two decades by the jeans revolution, tights, 'hot pants', and the mini-skirt. Many women just got out of the habit of wearing dresses and blouses, and the wardrobe of many young women today contains neither. The current vogue for wearing floral furnishings (itself a throwback to the late 60s) is undoubtedly a short-lived fashion, though skirts are certainly making a comeback in 1986.

Creative textile design in post-War Britain grew out of the Central School of Arts and Crafts in London. At a time when most designers were looking to Scandinavia for inspiration (a Scandinavia which in turn looked back to Chippendale, William Morris and the British Arts & Crafts Movement), a group of inspired design students spread a new design gospel, under the Head of the Textile Department named

Miss Batty. I was told by Mary Yonge, who taught part-time at the Central from 1946, that Miss Batty insisted on an industrial approach, at a time when the Royal College of Art supposedly produced teachers rather than designers. John Drummond went on from the Central to the RCA: Eduardo Paolozzi, the sculptor, invented original textured images and his most famous pupil, Terence Conran, went on to bigger things still. Gordon Crook stayed on to teach at the Central before moving to New Zealand. Audrey Tanner, who designed the 'Mandala' carpet — surely the most successful and longest lived Design Council Award winner of all time — was also there; as were Beryl Coles (to whom I will always be grateful) and Mary Oliver. Marianne Straub, a native of Switzerland who worked pre-War in Bradford, taught weaving there part-time whilst working for Warners at Braintree. There were others.

Their design style in the early 50s was based on a mixture of naturalism, textured effects, Paul Klee and photo-micrography (which became the basis for all decoration in the 1951 Festival of Britain), abstract with a simple linear basis. The Festival of Britain and its influence were a success beyond anyone's expectations and were to be the guiding spirit for design right through the Swinging Sixties to about 1973.

'Calyx' printed cotton design by Lucienne Day for Heals, 1951 (Courtesy of V & A Museum)

At this time (the early 50s), the firm of David Whitehead (no longer with us), under the design direction of an architect named John Murray, led the field with 'contemporary' designs, some by the painter Roger Nicholson — later to be appointed Professor of Textiles at the RCA. The word 'contemporary', which became the generic name for the style, was probably first coined by John Line and Company for a special collection of wallpapers.

Whilst most manufacturers stuck to the traditional designs that they thought they understood, a salesman named Tom Worthington created a business at the end of the War within the family firm of Heals, which became synonymous with the most avant-garde furnishing fabrics of the day. Tom, who was showman, opportunist and entrepreneur rolled into one, created a virtual stable of designers with Lucienne Day (ex-RCA and married to furniture designer Robin Day) as front-runner and Britain's answer to the famous Swedish designer, Astrid Sampe. To have a design in the Heals Fabric Collection was just about the finest accolade for any young designer. Among those to achieve it were Barbara Brown, Althea McNish, Robert Dodd, Fay Hillier, Doreen Dyall, Margaret Cannon, Nicola Wood and myself. In 1956 we all worked together as students in the same studio above the old Aeronautical Museum in Imperial Institute Road. We were followed later at the RCA by Natalie Gibson, Howard Carter (with his famous 'Sunflower' and 'Pansy' designs), Zandra Rhodes borrowing David Hockney's 'Medals', and Peter Hall, now in South Africa running Tongaat Textiles which was once David Whitehead SA.

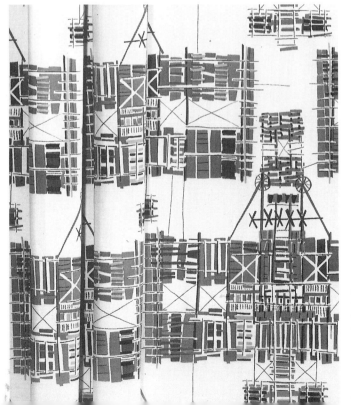

'Farnborough' textile design by Edward Pond, 1953 (Courtesy of Heal and Son)

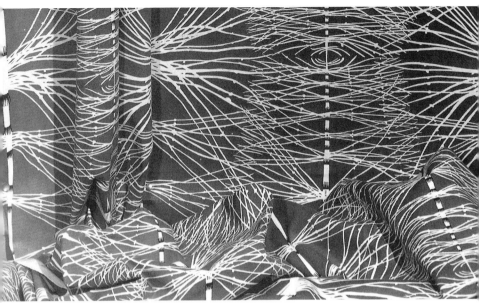

Howard Carter's 'Sunflower' was one of a number of designs which won a Cotton Board Award in 1962. The seven winning designs were 'allocated' to sponsoring manufacturers. Heals got 'Sunflower', which was an amazing success but which, in the normal way of things, they might never have had produced. The Manchester Cotton Board, under the inspired direction of Donald Tomlinson, started a number of designer promotions which eventually became the Texprint exhibitions and the forerunners of textile designers' fairs everywhere.

The teaching in the RCA Textile School — or, more accurately, the lack of it — did produce some amazing results. John Drummond and Humphrey Spender encouraged us, along with Margaret Leischner, a former Bauhaus student and Head of Weaving, who was succeeded some years later by Eileen Ellis (yet another ex-RCA student from that 1955–58 vintage). Weaving was still considered a bit arty crafty. We knew the work of Peter Simpson for Donald Brothers and the splendid woven fabrics by Edinburgh Weavers, and Tibor Reich, but that was about all. Power looms and knitting machines in art schools were still to come.

Hand screen printing is historically a relatively recent industrial process. First used in the USA in the 20s, it was not widely used in the UK until the end of the 30s, and then alongside block printing. When automatic screen printing arrived in the early 60s — first flat bed, and later rotary — block printing was finished and hand screen printing became an expensive speciality process. I was at Wardles in 1962 when Warners had their block-print designs transferred to automatic printed screens and remember the first trials being returned with instructions to 'put more printing mistakes in'. Block printing always contains slight fitting irregularities which give it its character, whilst screen printing is much more perfect.

Design creativity was directed at furnishing fabrics and wallpapers and sometimes carpets. Dress fabrics were ignored. Zandra Rhodes says in her autobiography that she was the first in her year at the RCA to design any dress fabrics.

Wallpapers are an important part of the story. In 1956, Crown introduced its famous 'Palladio' large-scale, hand screen printed collections. Based on an idea of Albert Hurst, Head of Crown Paints' Advisory Studio, they were first made at Lightbown Aspinall at Bred-

'Sicilian Lion' printed textile by Robert Nicholson, 1957 (Courtesy of Whitworth Art Gallery)

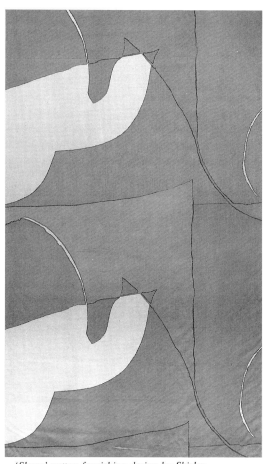

'Shape' cotton furnishing design by Shirley Craven for Hull Traders, 1966 (Courtesy of Whitworth Art Gallery)

bury near Stockport. Collections 1 – 6 were styled by Roger Nicholson, as were 'Palladio Magnus' (bigger than ever), 'Palladio Modus' (small scale for architects) and 'Palladio Mondo' (modern taste for the masses). Palladio, with Heals Fabrics, were to become synonymous with the best of British design, collecting the lion's share of Design Council Awards with the attendant free publicity. In 1963, the printing of 'Palladio' transferred from Lightbown Aspinall to Sandersons at Perivale. It was suggested that this was on the instructions of Mr Sanderson, then Chairman of The Wallpaper Manufacturers Limited and jealous of 'Palladio's' amazing design successes. A tearful Guy Busbyy, Design Director of Lightbowns, told me the news in the middle of Stockport in the winter of 1963. Palladio 7 was styled by Deryk Healey, and I styled 'Palladio's' Collections 8 and 9.

In the early 60s, the Ministry of Building and Public Works influenced the fabric trade by putting out tempting government tenders demanding high performance specification requirements, directed by a man named Eddie Hancock. As a result, really good original designs now appeared from any number of companies including Bernard Wardle, Margo, Textra and Cavendish Textiles (the John Lewis own brand), in competition with Heals, who had been getting most of the business. Cavendish Textiles is still run by Harry Davy who went into design partnership with fellow RCA weaving student Bill Brooke, and who both joined John Lewis together.

In 1960, Robin Gregson-Brown had left the textile department at RCA to join ICI Plastics Division at Hyde, Cheshire, where he styled the first Vymura collection for the domestic market, liberally based on Palladio. Vymura was the first PVC coated onto paper wallcovering collection anywhere. As a product type, this revolutionised the trade and helped the demise of the traditional wallpaper industry.

'Contemporary' had given way, in the late 50s, to textured designs as designers found a new god in Jackson Pollock and action painting. Doreen Dyall's desk at the RCA sat in a sea of encrusted varnish and paint, whilst other students dribbled and splashed paint all around, listening to Frank Sinatra's 'Songs for Swinging Lovers' and inspired by the soon to become famous RCA taschist painters, Dick Smith and Robin Denney, and by Michael Green (who set fire to his canvasses and painted with a bicycle). A sketch on action painting was a basic part of the programme of any RCA Christmas show with paint thrown liberally over the stage and the audience, usually by Dick Smith himself dressed up as Mathiea.

Shirley Craven, now a lecturer at Goldsmiths, also shared the same RCA textile studio, though she made her name with Hull Traders, a company founded by Tristram Hull which in the 60s challenged Heals' dominance as the leader of the avant garde. Later, under a new owner, Hull Traders sold a remarkable range of tubular cardboard furniture called Tomotom designed by Shirley's husband, Bernard Holdaway.

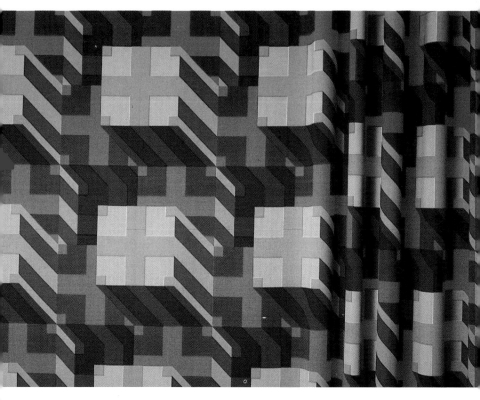

'Complex' textile design by Barbara Brown for Heals

Interior of Laura Ashley's Guildford shop, 1980

At this time, late 50s textile designers were much influenced by Rasch Wallpapers from Germany with techniques exploiting textures in new ways. The Wall Paper Manufacturers Limited, known as WPM, had exercised a monopolistic control over distribution in the UK wallpaper trade which prevented manufacturers outside the group from finding a retail market. The new Monopolies Commission's first target was WPM, destroying their control over the retail distribution of wallpaper, which started an erosion of that once great organisation that went on until Crown Wallpapers was sold to an American company in 1984. In 30 years, eight wallpaper factories closed including Sandersons and Lightbown Aspinall, plus the loss of the famous trade names like John Line and Shand Kydd. In 1965, WPM was taken over by Reed International with the result that over 20 years its 80% share of the total UK wallcoverings market was reduced to insignificance.

There were very few other outside influences where textiles styles were concerned. Fabrics from Germany by Pausa with designs derived from Renaissance paintings with bright colour and lots of texture were certainly different. Many artists designed fabrics — Moore, Scott, le Broquy and others — with only John Piper ever being really commercially successful. Cliff Holden, a Manchester-born painter living in Sweden, influenced design methods with innovative textured screen prints.

In the early 60s, Shirley Conran designed and put together a really interesting collection. Very much a 'one-off' collection, the designs and colourways were delightful. One design, a kind of saw edge stripe, hung in a restaurant in Blackheath Village for what must have been at least 20 years. Juliet Glynn-Smith, a graphic designer, came back from the USA to design for Conran in a very personal 'hem stitched edge' technique. One of her designs, based upon an Elizabethan embroidery issued as a postcard by the Victoria and Albert Museum, heralded the Victoriana look of the Swinging Sixties. Wardles 'Pandora' by Gillian Farr was in the same vein and must have been in continuous production for over 15 years from 1963. Another long-lived design of this type is John Lewis's 'Daisy Chain' by Pat Albeck (ex-RCA), a design quite obviously based upon William Morris's 'Blackthorn', still in production and still a bestseller. Pat Albeck is one of the UK's most successful and versatile textile designers. With her inimitable personal style, she manages to design successes from curtains to tea towels and tea cosies. Pat won one of the very first Cotton Board travel awards and went to Australia.

The Swinging Sixties, when it happened, did not really start until 1965, but then with an amazing crash of influences that was simply bewildering. The momentum built up slowly with the Beatles, Sandy Shaw, Dionne Warwick, 'That Was The Week That Was', and Carnaby Street. Op Art and Pop Art were established, but suddenly it all happened. The Rolling Stones, The Supremes, Percy Sledge, Edwin

Starr, The Chiffons, Little Stevie Wonder, mini-skirts, Art Nouveau, Art Deco, Voysey, William Morris, Bridget Reilly, Brigitte Bardot, Batman and Robin, James Bond, Habitat, King's Road, carrier bags, paper dresses, paper knickers, cardboard furniture, Polypops, Paperchase, Aretusa, Mr Freedom, Mr Feed'um, Bus Stop, Biba, Clobber, Ossie Clark, Mary Quant, and 'Puppet on a String' till you wanted to scream. And three funny painting students who came from the North to find fame and fortune in London — Binder, Edwards and Vaughan — kind of instant Kings of Pop Art. They painted Carnaby Street and Jimmy Saville's Rolls Royce with psychedelic patterns. All kinds of barriers broke down in the 60s and textile designers too became musicians, restauranteurs, furniture designers, fashion designers and photographers.

Flower Power was the spirit of the late 60s and its visual identity the 'flat floral'. Op Art died quickly. Pop Art lasted longer, particularly in graphics and products of all kinds. There was, for instance, a new interest in paper and paper things and cardboard furniture. Polypops introduced novel ideas in the use of cardboard and Art Deco graphics for giftwrap and tin trays. Very unusual corrugated cardboard toys for Polypops were designed by Roger Limbrick, yet another of that group of textile designers at the RCA from 1955 to 58. The tin tray kings were JRM, with many products designed by Ian Logan, a textile designer from the Central School who still designs metal boxes for his own company today. The Art Deco revival was a short-lived 'flash in the pan', though Liberty's revived some beautiful Art Deco, small-scale, bright geometric silk prints which look as nice now as they did then.

What really stayed the course and on into the 70s was Victoriana, Voysey and William Morris. The roots for this revival are to be found in the film sets by Cecil Beaton for 'My Fair Lady' which had interiors papered with Voysey designs made by Sandersons, which created a big demand. Sandersons continued to print William Morris wallpaper from original blocks and later introduced scaled down 'mini-Morris' and Wallpaper co-ordinates. A USA-based Japanese chain store, Azuma, used Voysey's 'Tulip and Bird' design for carrier bags in 1981, which took Art Nouveau back home after 100 years.

It was the carrier bag of the 60s which had the greatest significance and long-term design effect. Coloroll was a small paper carrier bag manufacturer with a factory 'up North' and a single, pokey office over Goodge Street station. In 1966, it introduced a small collection of bags designed by Jan Pienkowski of Gallery Five. They were bright and garish, based on Beardsley, William Morris and psychedelia. These bags were so successful that they became an international fashion accessory, exhibited at the Milan Triennale and on the cover of the *Director* magazine. Coloroll then diversified into greetings cards and wallpaper. Not very successfully at first, they dropped greetings cards and concentrated on wallcoverings using the same designs and flexographic printing as for the carriers. Flexography (printing with rubber rollers) proved to be an ideal print process for wallpapers which was taken up by the rest of the wallpaper trade. Novelty value created public interest and by 1975 Coloroll had grown into an important wallcovering company. Today, it is a public company with wallcoverings and textile interests and dominates the retail trade.

Co-ordination, the matching of furnishing fabrics with wallcoverings, had been a standard offer in the American 'decorator market' for many years. Sanderson Triad Collections were first in this country to use co-ordination as early as 1962. Among the early collections was a small surface print wallpaper design called 'Dimity', a small-scale all-over which is still a bestseller. Sandersons introduced other small-scale designs which created a fashion. In the mid 70s, Laura Ashley, a retail fashion business, started to print their own dress fabrics and later utilised spare printing capacity to make wallpaper using similar small-scale derivative designs until small-scale designs everywhere became known generically as 'Laura Ashley Prints'. Laura Ashley went public in 1985 on the back of their success in furnishings and wallpapers.

The swinging sixties came to an abrupt end in 1973 with the Middle East War and the subsequent oil crisis. The last Palladio-type collection was made in vinyl and called 'Pavilion', but big designs had had it by 73. Manufacturers and customers played safe as a need for security represented itself in chintzy cheerfulness and more and more small-scale co-ordination. From then until now design and colours have been 'cosy'.

Innovation, where it existed, was in bed linen, particularly with the advent of the duvet. Dorma, now part of Vantona Viyella, under the design direction of Sid Sykes lead the market. Dorma use modern marketing techniques and big names like Mary Quant and Marimekko, coupled with big advertising and promotion budgets, to stay in front. It is the small companies like Monitor Prints, that create the most unusual and innovative designs in this market though. In the UK we are blessed with any number of small companies who continually make bold design statements and influence fashion, but whose quantities and financial turnover are, unfortunately, of little or no consequence to the 'big boys'. Of these, Osborne and Little and Designers Guild (particularly Tessa Guild's involvement with Next) are among the most important. Skopos is a splendid advertisement for enterprise backing good design, quality and service. The Collier Campbell fabrics are beautifully designed and coloured, but made by Fisba, a Swiss company not even in the EEC! Maybe it is symptomatic of our malaise that the Design Council sells Fisba's nicely designed, but nevertheless foreign, fabrics in preference to British textiles.

For the past ten years, furnishing textiles have been dominated by the American look — Oriental-type landscapes and bouquets with birds in soft colours. Such designs seem to have an international appeal for use on upholstered furniture. Manufacturers are not tempted to try anything new and exciting when they see 101 versions of *The Diary of an Edwardian Lady* and Laura Ashley-types making the bestseller lists.

Forty years ago, it would not have been too much to expect that a few British designers and manufacturers would have an international reputation by 1986, but where are they, or where did they go? We have no Marimekko, Jack Lenor Larsen, Boris Kroll, Boussac, Schumacher, Cantoni Baumann. The contract market for furnishing fabrics is almost dominated by foreign manufacturers, particularly in expensive printed silks, pile fabrics and intricate jacquards. Something is wrong somewhere. When Canary Wharf, the commercial development of London's docklands, gets built, it will have been designed by Americans and filled with continental furniture and furnishings. The carpets will probably be British and maybe the wallcoverings. The UK wallcoverings industry may have been through some changes but it is still dominant. If we could only say the same for the textile industry!

The problem is that while the UK textile industry is still large and important, its product mix is still production/commodity orientated. Fibres, yarns, plains, linings, backings, fillings, dyestuffs and so on, with design just another part of it all which few people at the top understand or care about. The old patriarchal management system which made Morton, Sanderson and Sekers, has gone, obviously creating opportunities for the new patriarchs like Conran, Osborne and Little, Designers Guild, Bodymap and Interior Selection. Without doubt, the biggest change to come is within the new own-branding of retail chains like Next, Now and Warehouse, carrying on from Habitat and Laura Ashley. What will the likes of Marks and Spencer, John Lewis, Boots, Sainsburys and Tesco do to keep up with these new retailing developments? If anything has happened its that 'design' has arrived. Questions in Parliament, television programmes, the subject is talked of as a positive government panacea. For certain, standards of public taste have risen beyond expectation and it is now possible to buy well designed fabrics and wallpapers almost anywhere. Unfortunately, it all happened just a bit too late.

A change in the economic climate and we might make it next time.

'Six Views'
furnishing fabrics
by Collier Campb

BRITISH PRODUCT DESIGN 1946–86

THE CHANGING RELATIONSHIP BETWEEN DESIGNER AND
MANUFACTURER — A PERSONAL VIEW
MARY ALEXANDER INTERVIEWS KENNETH GRANGE

ALEXANDER
You were 17 in 1946, what are your personal recollections of the Britain Can Make It exhibition?

GRANGE
For me the abiding memory was not so much the *product* as the *presentation*. You have to remember that, at that time, nobody was used to conspicuous design, particularly design that didn't have a war propaganda message, and to walk into a hall which was all peaceable and all pleasure was a very striking experience. In fact I think that the memory was more to do with the promise of the thing and the design of the environment, rather than the actual objects. Much more significant in my view, was what actually transpired between 1946 and the 1951 Festival of Britain, because I'm convinced that many people still don't fully appreciate the extent to which product design as such was stimulated by the Festival.

The exhibition became the basis for commissioning many pieces of furniture. Ernest Race, for example, was producing quite unexpected new types of modern furniture, based on previous experiments with new materials and construction techniques.

Eric Marshall's 'Bermuda' TV, late 1950s

97

I particularly remember the excitement generated pre-1951 by a new range of tables and chairs he designed which used aluminium castings for the principal parts. A very sophisticated hollow-section plastic material called Holoplast, with a veneered upper surface, was used for the table top with cast aluminium legs, resulting in a very elegant modernist piece of furniture.

How would you describe the mood or spirit of that period which gave rise to such a richness of design innovation?

'Peaceable dynamism' would do. What I think is interesting is that designers such as Wells Coates, Christian Barman, Jack Howe, Douglas Scott, Joseph Emberton and that group of people were bringing modern product ambitions from the pre-War period into the 1950s. Many of these were very sophisticated in terms of product innovation, and I don't think we see anything nearly as sensational today.

I personally have a very fond memory of that post-War period as being very dynamic in terms of product design, and they were products you could actually buy in the shops. British manufacturers such as HMV, Murphy Radios, EK Cole and Ultra had an understanding and a vision of what industrial design as a discipline was all about. For example, HMV commissioned some very exciting and elegantly modelled irons, and a chromium electric heater which was a landmark in design innovation. Eric Marshall's 'Bermuda' TV design for Ultra broke new design ground in the perceived size of the cabinet design, and the electric heaters from EK Cole look modern today.

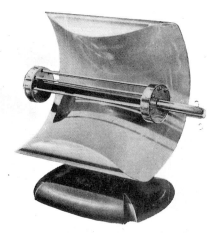

THE *Bruton* REFLECTOR FIRE

HMV's Bruton reflector fire, 1946 (Courtesy of Thorn EMI Archives)

In the late 1940s and 50s there were a clutch of British products which, in my view, were world leaders in terms of design, style, taste and judgement. It would be an interesting study to examine the patterns of growth, merger and acquisition of the British electrical companies, and to consider what happened to all that design enterprise which, had it been sustained, would have put Britain in the forefront of design innovation. For various reasons this all got lost in the 1970s.

Do you think the European émigrées in Britain exerted a particular influence on design and manufacturers' attitudes at this time?

Yes, in some specifics. I think that the refugee designers and architects were a very important influence, especially in architecture and display design, and their adventurous display designs for the Festival of Britain and marvellous window and shop front designs in London had a profound effect on young designers for the next ten or fifteen years. Also it must be remembered that, at that time, Scandinavia was viewed as a cornucopia of modern design, and many British architects, including Jack Howe who I went to work for, used to make an annual 'pilgrimage' there to see the latest modern buildings.

Looking back to the work for your early clients, what do you see as the main changes that have occurred concerning the kinds of people you dealt with, and the size, structure and organisation of those companies?

My first client, Kodak, came to me through a chance contact and the other two, Kenwood and Venner, were referred to me via the Design Council, which played an important co-ordinating role between manufacturer and designer in the years following the Festival of Britain.

Kodak had a very highly organised, extremely sophisticated management structure with a very mature engineering capability. As a young designer, they gave me an education, although I reciprocated by offering them new design ideas which were put into production. For example, I designed for them the first camera which ever made money as a camera rather than merely as a means of selling film. Interestingly, it was pure good fortune that I got the job because they had previously decided against employing an industrial designer after a bad experience, but presumably they found in me a younger and more manageable person and I was very respectful of them, so we got on well and it grew into a close relationship which lasted for more than 20 years.

Kenwood, on the other hand, was not nearly so structured as a company, and was run absolutely as an autocracy by Kenneth Wood, an attractive entrepreneur and salesman. However, they were a much less sophisticated firm at that time, and as a young designer I was thrown into the deep end of debate, negotiation and argument with the draftsmen working on the product. I didn't have much to do with the management at that time, because each time I designed a product I made the presentation directly to Kenneth Wood. I remember those early years with the company as a very ambitious, dynamic and flowering time which I enjoyed immensely. Kenneth Wood was prepared to proceed with new products at a rate of knots on the strength of the commercial success of the Chef. Other new products followed which were immensely successful, we couldn't manufacture them fast enough to meet demand.

Kenneth Wood had certain ideas about product quality and consumer service which established the reputation of the company and still remain the case today. For example, he firmly believed in making a product of very high manufacturing integrity so that its longevity was never in question. He was also strongly committed to the concept of service and employed a fleet of vehicles which would respond to a call within 24 hours regardless of geographical distance. In the long term, this did the company enormous good because the Kenwood brand name became synonymous with unchallenged high quality consumer service and good value.

The third client, Venner, is an interesting example of a company that was not primarily interested in design. Venner were well established manufacturers of excellent time mechanisms, and showed great foresight at that time in anticipating the future demand in this country for the American parking meter concept. They negotiated a deal with the leading US company to manufacture the existing design in Britain, but their request for approval from the Department of Transport was refused on the recommendation of the Design Council owing to the poor aesthetic design of the product. Since the deal had already been negotiated, Venner were forced to follow the Design Council's recommendation and employ an industrial designer to improve the existing product. So that was how I became involved in designing a case around the existing mechanism, although the client had not made a free choice to employ a designer.

Therefore I was dealing with three quite different types of client. Today, Venner by sheer force of the publicity given to design would probably employ a designer, but I have no idea if they would be anything like as open or generous in their brief and in giving the designer the benefit of the doubt as being the best judge, as would the Kodak or Kenwood of today. This reflects quite simply on the products made by these different companies. The Venner product is sold primarily on its specification and often not to the discriminating public. Indeed in the case of an engineering component of a system such as street lighting the judgement will be made by a single purchasing engineer. Not surprisingly, that person is rarely knowledgeable about design.

I think that, in retrospect, one of the main differences is that at the time I'm talking about, a client like Kodak were being philanthropic in their design approach. They already had such a hold on the marketplace that they didn't really *need* to invest in the kind of innovative design I was doing at that time. The main point is that they *believed* the product should be better by design. Although Kodak were paying me small design fees, they were also generous as clients and suggested that I should be paid a retainer as their consultant which was not usual at that time.

The motivation of a client in employing a designer varies and depends on the type of industry. For example, if you're in the fashion or furniture business the design and style is very much more important, because the potential buyer is going to be very concerned about its appearance and handling qualities. On the other hand, if your product is judged purely in terms of cost and mechanical function as a Venner timing device which lives its life in the dirty, rusty confines of a street lighting column, then improving that product in terms of making it more pleasurable is not a high priority in terms of capital spent.

Have the methods of dealing with management and staff in a company such as Kenwood changed much between then and now?
No, not much, but we as designers have learned a lot more and perhaps now take more initiative in the designer–client relationship. For example, today we might conceive an uncommissioned idea for a client and take it along for presentation. Although it was open to me to have done that then, I was so busy and Kenwood's own in-house design staff were also initiating new ideas, so there didn't seem to be a pressing need for me to push them forward.

Do you think that management decisions about product design and development tend to be more committee-bound today?
Yes, certainly. I think that the government of industry by bureaucracy has been one of the major changes during the past 20 years. Historically

it is interesting to look at how Kenwood as a small company was taken over by Thorn, a large corporation, which had no option but to run the company as a broader democracy. Whereas in the 1950s and 60s design presentations were made directly to Kenneth Wood, today they are channelled through numerous levels of management and decisions are made in a large forum.

Was this part of a general pattern of change that was taking place in British manufacturing industry in the 1970s?

I think it was to do with peoples' ages, attitudes and career ambitions at that particular moment in time. I suspect that if you were to take a broader overview of British manufacturing industries in the post-War period, you would find that many were started up by men who came out of the forces in their late 20s and early 30s, who were entrepreneurial in spirit and had a small amount of capital to start up a business. It's also important to remember that industry was really hungry for products at that time.

As I see it, the late 1960s and 70s saw a profound change in the structure or perhaps in the balance of power in industry. This was the period of asset-stripping and making money by being economic rather than by actually being innovative or dynamic. Asset stripping suddenly became a reputable profession with profound future consequences for design and investment in product innovation. The financial movement dominated the industrial management philosophy of that time, and appeared to offer a bright new wave of industrial organisation to young ambitious managers. I suspect that was when a number of motivated people moved into senior management positions in industry and that's when the movement of *management by money* started.

I witnessed this happen to one of my clients, Henry Hope and Sons, a fine manufacturing company based in the Midlands. The company was run by cultivated people who really appreciated what fine paintings and fine glass were, and who exercised visual discrimination in developing their products. But while I was still working for them, the company was spotted by a well known asset stripping company, the value of its assets were identified, and suddenly the factory was closed down. This pattern of 'economic rehabilitation' of small companies by various well known asset stripping machines was fairly common in the 1970s and was not viewed as in any way immoral.

Do you think there are any parallels to be found in the design attitudes and motivation of clients in the 1980s and those of today?

Yes, there are interesting similarities. Today I think it's widely recognised that asset stripping was a relatively short-term gain, like a radical piece of surgery that was temporarily necessary. But you can't just go on pruning, because there's an awful lot of new planting that has to be done and *temperamentally* those people are not the best ones to do the planting.

I think that there has been a very interesting revolution in marketing attitudes recently, and designers are now reaping the benefits. About ten years ago, financial managers in this country, looking at developments in the USA concerning how new products were researched and developed, began to discover *marketing* in the sense of a more carefully researched and disciplined way of deciding what products should be developed.

This new generation of marketing people, against all the norms of the time, were highly rewarded in salaries, authority, glamorous image and career expectations. It is these people who, in a sense, have inherited the world, but the difference in the 1980s is that they now recognise that *design* is at the centre of it. I think there is a parallel in the temperament of the people who are now at the top of these companies, although I don't yet see the same level of entrepreneurial determination that there was in the post-War years.

What other recent changes would you identify as being important in the designer–client relationship, and how do these impinge on your work today?

It is noticeable that companies which were previously finance dominated are gradually showing signs of change. Although finance still reigns as king in the boardroom, marketing staff — who tend to be more broad viewed and pragmatic in approach — are assuming greater status within manufacturing companies and it is these people who perceive a wider role for design in identifying new business opportunities for the company. In my view, the natural home of design is with the making of the goods, and there is an urgent need in this country to upgrade the rewards of the people involved in the activity of manufacturing. But the best situation today is where design is the ally of marketing, resulting in a high calibre of product, skilfully targeted towards identified consumer needs. Financial investment in design is often perceived by financial directors as a risk, but historically one must ask why senior management in this country have found it easier to allocate large financial budgets to advertising departments while starving design and development departments of the investment necessary to produce innovative, commercially successful products. If a manufacturing company does not have a strong, innovative engineering design unit, then it becomes merely a merchant and its infrastructure is destroyed.

I am currently a design director of two major British consumer manufacturing companies, and attend board meetings as a matter of right, not just when senior management consider it to be relevant. My position as consultant designer and design director is a relationship which does not come easily and has to be worked at. I see the role of design director as one of raising the level and quality of design in all the company's products, of evaluating the product range, and of working collaboratively with the company's in-house design team. In this way, the consultant design director is able to assist the position and influence of the internal designers, and I can represent the views of the development director to the chief executive in a context that is not coloured by internal company politics.

Finally, there is a tendency today for managers in manufacturing industry to be educated more narrowly than their counterparts 15 or 20 years ago. One interesting effect of this is that the brighter the young manager, the greater is the tendency for him to question the designer's expertise on design issues. On the other hand, one of the good things about this is that it does actually force the designer to be more articulate and think more carefully about what he is saying. I think that I tend to employ more analogies and use wit a bit more. I don't think this necessarily makes the product any better designed, but it does make the social intercourse a bit more entertaining — and of course that's one of the benefits of getting older because people are more willing to listen to you and you find yourself in a forum that you wouldn't have had access to before — and moreover, not only allowed in but given a seat of privilege. I enjoy that aspect very much and it does put you on your metal.

Although I see very encouraging signs today of a positive re-appraisal of the role of design, senior management must also be prepared to fund *non-specific* conceptual design work for future invest-ment. In the final analysis, it depends on a management determination to pursue the uneasy course of achieving product excellence rather than adequacy, and excitement more than mere interest. The consequence of these ambitions is more effort, nuisance and frequently additional cost, but in my experience it is this that gets a company's products into a leadership position.

All in all we need the thoughtful skills of today with the flair and philanthropy of yesterday — what you're talking about is investment in creativity!

Advertisement promoting investment in design designed by Geoffrey Fisher

DESIGN AND THE BRITISH CONSUMER ELECTRICAL AND ELECTRONICS INDUSTRY: THORN EMI

PENNY SPARKE

Great Britain is not, generally speaking, highly rated for the design of its consumer electrical and electronic goods. Lasting myths about 'wood effect' television sets and 'coal effect' electric fires, designed to appeal to a conservative mass market, are deeply embedded within the contemporary picture of British design in this area. In the 1920s and 30s, when the USA leapt clearly ahead, we were slow in developing our manufacturing industries and, in the post-War years, Japan, Germany, Holland and Italy have left us behind on both the technological and the design fronts. Our position therefore, in an international context, is far from strong. It would be unfair and unwise to dismiss British efforts in the field of technology altogether but, from a design point of view (as a recent article in *Design* [June 1985] suggested), we do have some problems both domestically and on the world market.

These views about Britain's electrical and electronic consumer goods have been well and extensively aired and, short of initiating an expensive and intensive campaign aimed at reforming British manufacturers' attitudes towards design, little can be done in the immediate future. It is, however, worth looking at the way the relationship between industry and design has evolved in the past few decades to see whether the usual explanation concerning the lack of taste in the British mass market constitutes the whole picture, or whether there are additional reasons why, in 1986, we take such a conservative approach, on the whole, towards the design of our consumer electronics.

Thorn EMI is the last remaining major manufacturer of consumer electricals and electronics in the UK. It has achieved this position primarily through the acquisitive nature of the late Sir Jules Thorn who, from the 1920s onwards, set out to buy up as many companies as he possibly could in similar technological and manufacturing areas to his own. By the mid 1980s the company has diversified into areas such as TV rentals and manufacture; domestic appliances, lighting; information technology; defence; security; music; X-ray scanning and radar. Only three sections — TV, lighting and domestic appliances — are involved with the consumer market.

Thorn is not a company without problems at the moment, both financial and organisational, the main one being the question of its identity. Because of the somewhat ad hoc manner in which smaller companies have been absorbed by Thorn over the years it tends, as a whole, to have a low public profile while the names of the smaller firms it has taken over (such as Bendix, Tricity, Moffat and Parkinson Cowan in the domestic appliance sector) are better known. The fact that the parent company's logo appears on all its products seems to make little difference. This is hardly surprising since the logo, a simple combination of the earlier Thorn and EMI symbols, was the result of a committee decision rather than that of a consultant designer concerned with the corporate image of the company.

This is a problem that has existed for many years and that is being tackled in an evolutionary rather than a radical manner. Back in the 1950s, for instance, the radio and TV section operated under a number of seperate brands, namely Ferguson, HMV, Marconi and, a little later, Ultra. This meant the duplication of numerous facilities (including design skills) and, inevitably, a dilution of promotional spending. Today they are unified under the Ferguson label, the name of the radio company which Thorn acquired in 1936 and which set it in that direction. In the industrial sector there is a move afoot to 'Thorn EMI' everything but this has yet to extend to those areas — appliances — which have day-to-day contact with the consumer. The question of design in the sense of corporate image lies, therefore, at the very heart of Thorn's current difficulties.

Lessons can be learnt about the question of the general relationship between design and industry by looking back at Thorn EMI's past as it subsumes the stories of many of Britain's leading appliance and radio and TV manufacturers. The two major branches of the present parent company, Thorn and EMI, which came together in 1979, had distinct but similar histories. The Gramophone Company is best remembered for one of its brand names, 'His Master's Voice', which is associated in many people's minds with Francis Barrow's 'Nipper' the dog. EMI thus goes back as far as the invention of recorded sound. The Thorn Electrical Company started out, however, as the Electric Lamp Service Company, and was established in the late 1920s by Jules Thorn, a middle European who came over to Britain selling light bulbs. In 1936 he bought Ferguson, a radio company, and moved into manufacturing in that field. (Domestic appliances were added with the acquisition of Tricity in 1951.) In the 1930s the Gramophone Company also moved into the production of radio-gramophones and electrical goods, using the HMV label, and, with the advent of television in the middle of that decade, ventured into the manufacture of TV consoles as well. The first, made in 1937, was a modification of an existing radiogram but later models were designed especially for this new medium. The Marconiphone label was linked to the Gramophone Company at this time as well. At Britain Can Make It a Gramophone Company TV console was on display along with some Thorn lighting and a double-pointed iron, called the 'Mary Ann' which was made by a small electrical company that Thorn had recently purchased.

Several of the small domestic appliances exhibited in 1946 with the HMV label indicated the progressive attitude that the company had demonstrated in the 1930s through its commissions to leading consultant designers of the day, including Christian Barman. Notable among them were the little 'Bruton' reflector fire, which was described as having a 'modern appearance' and a 'distinctive design'; the 'Belgrave' fire which was considered 'an outstanding example of what can be accomplished by careful thought to the question of eye-appeal' and the 'Controlled Heat' iron (designed in 1937), an elegant exercise in streamlining, which was sold as being 'designed by a sculptor for the contour of the relaxed human hand'. When Thorn took over the HMV and Marconiphone labels in 1957 their earlier reputations for design innovation were diminished.

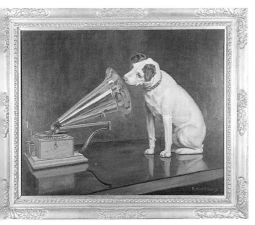

Original painting of 'Nipper the Dog' (Courtesy of EMI Music Archives)

Range of 1940s heaters for EMI (Courtesy of Thorn EMI Archives)

Part of the reason for this lay in the changing nature of the British market for consumer electricals from the pre- to the post-War years. While, before 1939 such products were the preserve of a fairly affluent sector of society, after the War they became much more widely available. This meant that at the very moment when Thorn moved its interests from lighting to consumer appliances and TV (Ferguson produced its first TV console in 1946), it had to deal with the problem of catering for a new mass market. Between 1948 and 1953 huge advances in TV production were made due to increased public interest and, by the end of the 1950s, Thorn led the way in TV production in Britain, having either destroyed or absorbed most of its competitors. Inevitably the emphasis on design was replaced by a concentration on price as that was the most important factor for most of the new consumers. In addition both radio and TV had strong links with the traditional furniture industry. These objects played an important role in the living area of the house and therefore took on the appearance of furniture items, a fact which tended to reinforce their conservative aesthetic. In the production of radios and TVs in the 1940s and 50s, the chassis was made first. It was then inserted into a wooden box which was designed and made by a cabinet-maker: only the Bakelite handles gave away the fact that it was a modern product. Staff members at EMI recall that there was a small cabinet-makers's shop on their premises at Hayes and Mr R E Norman, who has been with Ferguson for 40 years and is now one of Thorn EMI's directors, remembers that freelance cabinet-makers were used to provide the wooden cases for radios and TVs. He pointed out, also, that there was a much higher degree of flexibility for variation in design at that time as cabinet-makers could use veneers in countless different decorative ways. With the later advent of injection moulding as the main production technique that flexibility was inevitably lost.

In contrast with companies such as Ekco and Murphy, which commissioned well known architects to design pieces for them, Thorn was, from the early post-War years, clearly more concerned with meeting the needs of the mass market than with design innovation. The company showed no interest in the progressive experiments of other firms and kept its eye on what it considered to be 'mass taste', sticking with wood and the furniture image, not only because they fulfilled consumer expectations but also because tooling costs were low (which is partly why wood is still used in the manufacture of the larger TV sets, only now, of course, it is chipboard covered with 'wood effect' plastic laminate).

Price, rather than design, was undoubtedly the priority in Thorn's radio and TV production through the 1950s and 60s. One of the reasons why the mass of the British public was so receptive to these goods was, according to Mr Norman, that it had been object-starved during the War and was ready, therefore, to buy almost anything, provided that it was new. Britain was short of things for much longer than most other countries, such as Germany and Italy which resumed manufacturing on a larger scale much more quickly than Britain. It is important, also, to remember that radio, and especially TV, were new products and therefore sold on novelty value alone. Their very availability had enormous sales appeal. The emphasis, where TVs were concerned, on renting rather than buying also tended to reinforce Thorn's conservative approach towards the appearance of its products.

The country which led the way where consumer electricals and electronics were concerned in the 1940s and 50s was the USA. Mr Norman remembers it as the 'home of industry' and it was with American companies, in particular Philco and Sylvania, that Thorn sought to forge links at that time. American industry was organised on a mass production basis and it made huge advances in plastics technology during the War. It was a model that Thorn set out to emulate and, in 1949, it introduced compression moulding which was used first on a nine-inch table TV.

Radio design from the 1940s for EMI showing continued use of wood veneer (Courtesy of Thorn EMI Archives)

With this innovation Thorn committed itself to large-scale, high-volume production. Injection moulding was introduced in the late 1950s for transistor radios which, with their aluminium trim, owed much to the style emanating from Detroit. What was missing, however, was a parallel commitment to mass marketing — the other, essential, side of the coin where the American model was concerned. Without mass marketing Thorn could not lead the way and produce a highly standardised economical product; it had to still fulfil the vagaries of what it considered to be public taste. This omission was a crucial one.

Inevitably, though, the introduction of new production techniques and the transition from low- to high-cost tooling modified the role that design played within the company. An in-house design team was employed from the late 1940s onwards, although, as Mr Norman points out, the services of the cabinet-makers were not totally dispensed with until the end of the following decade. Both radiograms and the larger TVs remained 'furniturised' until then — a fact which had much to do

Radio design for Ferr
with Bakelite case, 193
(Courtesy V & A Mus

with the attitude of the British public towards the role of technology in the home at that time. Unused to the new gadgets with which the American market had been familiar since the 1930s, the bulk of the British buyers were wary about the intrusion of these objects into their homes. They tended, on the whole, still to think of TVs and radiograms as items of furniture and preferred the large bulky pieces to the lighter, more contemporary designs which were produced by companies such as Ekco and Murphy. In 1946 R D Russell commented on the fact that 'as furniture, radiograms are disappointing when compared to contemporary or antique furniture'.

Thorn EMI has pursued a general policy of keeping its divisions fairly separate from each other from a marketing point of view but has had, at the same time, to standardise much of its production. Thus today, for example, Tricity and Kenwood manufacture their microwave cookers in the same factory but design and market them separately and Parkinson Cowan and Main's gas cookers are also made in the same plant but sold under separate brand names. Because this has not been rationalised with a central design facility, this tends to mean that design variations are highly superficial and depend upon surface additions and details. Back in the 1960s a few companies took on board the principles of standardisation from a design perspective and tried to evolve designs which exploited that principle but which allowed for variation by introducing a range of related products. As Kenneth Grange has already noted, the Ultra radio and TV company was one of the most successful firms in proposing a family of products for mass production. Aware that, at the end of the 1950s, the demand for radios and TVs was declining sharply, Eric Marshall introduced his elegant and much praised 'Bermuda' TV and 'Rio' transistor radio. He was moving towards a position in which he would be responsible for the firm's entire corporate image. Thorn took Ultra over in 1961 at the height of its success with its new products. A writer in *Design* magazine in January 1962 was optimistic about the take-over as he saw the

*'Ultra' Radio design
by Eric Marshall,
1958*

possibility of large-scale manufacture solving all the problems of superficial style changes, claiming that 'the rationalisation of production that could result from the present regrouping of the industry will provide an opportunity for investment in tooling for longer runs. This in itself should tend to work against the idea of the annual model change and the need to use standard knobs and handles which often are unrelated to the rest of the designs.'

Needless to say this dream was never realised due to pressures from the market, to Thorn's lack of confidence in breaking away from what it felt to be the needs of the British public, and to its decision neither to go for complete standardisation with design in a central role nor to integrate its acquisitions into a single identity.

Along with Ultra the other company with a high design profile to be acquired by Thorn in the 1980s was Kenwood, taken over in 1968. Formed in 1947 by Kenneth Wood, the firm started out manufacturing toasters and then moved into the production of streamlined foodmixers which owed much to Sunbeam's model, available on the British market at that time.

In the early 1960s the British consultant designer, Kenneth Grange, was approached by Kenwood to design a new foodmixer and the elegant, sophisticated product he came up with — the Chef — remains one of Britain's strongest designs from that decade. Kenwood's strength lay in its modest size, in its forceful and far-sighted management, in its unified image and in its commitment to design. Thorn EMI has kept its name as a distinct brand but some of the energy went out of the company with the withdrawal of Kenneth Wood as its guiding light. Kenneth Grange has, however, recently been appointed to the Board of Thorn's domestic appliance section, a decision which will undoubtedly help give design a higher profile within the company. He has been involved in the design of Tricity's most advanced electric cooker and, in addition to his continued work for Kenwood's products — among them the 'Spring' fizzy drinks dispenser — is likely to play a role in

111

encouraging Thorn EMI to consider design, like research, as a more centralised process.

Twenty years ago, claims Mr Norman, Britain was prepared to accept a product with a less costly design than either Germany or France. Designing for export meant simply copying the goods of foreign competitors, Grundig in Germany for example. Emulation is, regrettably, still a policy which Thorn pursues today, only now the main competitors are the Japanese. The company is aware, however, that appearance design has played a much more vital role within the manufacture and marketing of goods in the past 15 years than ever before. This is largely a result of the increased competition from Japanese producers and the absence of a captive domestic market such as existed back in the 1940s and 50s. Within Ferguson there is now a much closer link between design and marketing: the design team has, fairly recently in fact, moved its allegiance from the technical to the commercial director.

Another area of fairly new activity within Ferguson is the commitment to market research which was initiated about ten years ago. The company organises what it calls 'haul tests' which take place on shopping precincts on Saturday afternoons. Shoppers are presented with a range of alternative products, mostly from competitors with their brand names covered, along with some proposed new projects by Thorn. The results are fed into all future design decisions. It is a policy which presents problems on one level inasmuch as it means that all new products are market-led, leaving no room for innovation or for taking the unprecedented step of creating a new market.

Thorn EMI has a massive centralised research facility but there is not much thought given to relating it to design innovation. EMI's research laboratories, which first opened in 1927, bear witness to the pioneering research work that the company has undertaken over the past 60 years, from innovations in stereo sound recording to X-ray scanning techniques. Thorn has also made numerous technological breakthroughs. In the area of lighting, for instance, it has made a name for itself with several ingenious advances: in 1967 it introduced the first solid-state colour television, and it has recently applied its discoveries in halogen lighting to cooking as well. The domestic appliance section continues, however, with only one or two exceptions, to produce cookers which lack the visual flair of foreign competitors.

In conclusion, much of Thorn's essential conservatism in product design is a result of the scale of its operations and its inability to find ways of combining standardisation with market variation in other than the most superficial of ways. Ironically, 40 years ago, when it was a much smaller concern and when cabinet-makers made the TV and radio boxes, flexibility was easier and it was possible to maintain quality while meeting the needs of a variegated market. When that market got bigger and new materials were introduced, however, Thorn dropped its standards, and failed to learn the lesson that Ultra was offering it. Today, once more, as a writer in a recent *Design* magazine has commented, 'the market place is fragmenting and changing all the time' and as he added, 'years have been wasted on a futile attempt to compete on the basis of price'. Ferguson has recently had financial problems and Stan Lee, chief designer there, is convinced of the need to put more emphasis on design. Only with design as a central element within production and marketing can the needs of 'variety and originality' be satisfactorily met.

It is easy to blame British manufacturers in the area of consumer electricals and electronics for their present difficulties. It is easy too to forget that they have evolved in the way they have for a number of reasons, many of them outside their control: primary among these is the essential conservatism of the domestic market. However, Thorn's programme of continued acquisition and expansion, linked with its lack of a unified identity and its general anonymity; its failure to develop sophisticated mass marketing techniques when they were first needed; its dependence upon 'market-led' decisions; and its continued emphasis upon price as a main selling factor have combined to make it a company with a low design profile today. In spite of the early advances of such companies as HMW, Ultra and Kenwood, we are left with a confused consumer electronics industry which is finding it increasingly hard to compete with Japan. It is an object lesson for all those manufacturers which have followed the same pattern in the four decades since the War.

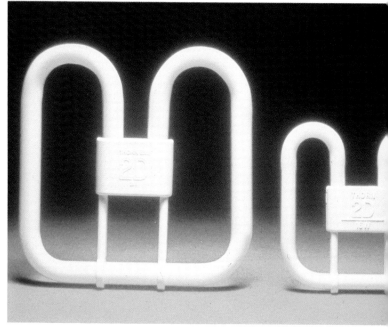

Innovative, energy-saving 2D Halogen light bulbs from Thorn EMI

Part 5

Retailing and Design

The fifth part of this book moves away from design as a process towards its role in the distribution and consumption of goods. It highlights, in particular, the way in which the changing structure of retailing goods in this country has, in the period since 1946, affected the nature of the products bought and sold. Anne Gardener, a historian of modern design who graduated recently from the Royal College of Art, tackles the question of the changes in fashion retailing and the concomitant effect on design and taste in the period in question. It was an area which influenced the retailing patterns of a number of other, less ephemeral products such as furniture, as my essay on the furniture retailer as taste-maker sets out to establish. This chapter aims to fill a gap in recent accounts of design in Britain in this period.

FASHION RETAILING 1946-86
ANNE GARDENER

The business of making and selling clothes has altered radically in the past 40 years, and the main direction of change — from independent retailers to chain stores; from the craftsmanship of couture to mass-production — reflects the ways in which British society, commerce and industry have also changed. The movement has generally been one of great expansion, but clothing as a commodity maintains an unusually intimate relationship with its market: social attitudes, status and class are reflected in how people dress while the means of supplying that market demonstrate the levels of mass-manufacturing, marketing and distribution present in the industry. Most significantly of all, the 40 years since the end of the Second World War have seen the development of a highly organised consumer society. The advantages of a better education, regular wages and increased leisure time have meant that a very large section of society has been able to enjoy consumption for its own sake. After food, magazines and popular entertainment, clothing has become one of the most disposable commodities and fashion is the motivation for change.

Selling clothes has become big business; selling fashion, even bigger business. Retailing clothes which change continually according to notions of what is fashionable is the capitalist's dream, as built-in obsolescence naturally strengthens the economic momentum and growth of the industries involved. But it can also be a manufacturer's major headache. Failure to plan, predict and pre-empt fashion change has been the downfall of many companies — particularly independent manufacturers and retailers without the resources to change gear or direction every time fashion does.

However, despite the obvious economic relationship between fashion and the selling of clothes in the post-War period, most histories of fashion and retailing covering the past 40 years concentrate on issues of design and styling in clothes without looking at the economic mechanism beneath. For example, much is made of British couture design in the 1950s — Hardy Amies and Norman Hartnell — and the pop boutique boom of the 1960s — Mary Quant and Biba. While both these areas were very important in design terms, they also have great significance for the development of fashion retailing. At the same time little mention is usually made of the massive growth in mail order and multiple chain stores as venues for selling clothes and fashion to an enormous number of consumers. So, while there have been many changes, it should be recognised that they have had more to do with the structure of the fashion and textile industries, the development of a mass consumer market and new techniques in marketing and retailing than with specific phases of creative activity on the part of individuals. Creative design works at the centre of the fashion industry but it is a combination of the other factors which brings the product — clothing — to the consumer.

Before considering the period in more detail, it is worth summarising the main ways in which the retailing of fashion has altered, and some of the reasons behind those changes. Later, some suggestions will be put forward as to how the development of retailing affected popular notions of taste and the implications for British design in the retailing of fashion.

Most noticeably since the War, there have been increasing supplies of mass-produced medium-quality garments on the market. Much of the immediate improvement in quality and the standardisation of cloth was due to precedents set by the wartime Utility clothing scheme and the rationalisation of clothing production. The 1950s saw the growth of a number of large manufacturing companies employing advanced, sectionalised production techniques for cutting out and making up: an Eastman cutter could cut out up to 200 layers of cloth at a time. This allowed large bulk orders of an even standard and quality to be produced efficiently and economically. Company amalgamations and take-overs in the textile industry during the late 1950s and early 60s resulted in a number of major companies with integrated manufacturing and retailing interests: Courtaulds, Carrington Viyella and Montague Burton are particular examples.

Courtaulds, as a textile company, acquired control of a number of clothing manufacturers producing brand-named goods with an existing and assured market, while Marks & Spencer, primarily retailers, contracted manufacturers to make up bulk orders for sale under the St Michael label. The development of multiple chain stores as retail outlets for mass-produced medium-quality clothing has been the natural extension of this system. Finally, the whole system of marketing and retailing fashion has grown in complexity. Intensive advertising through women's magazines and fashion editorials in newspapers has stimulated a greater awareness of fashion changes among a wider audience of consumers. Marketing and sales techniques increasingly exploited the purchasing power of new markets and consumer groups like teenagers. In all these ways the whole structure of demand can be seen to have expanded enormously. As one historian noted in 1957,

Before the war, the demand for medium-quality clothing was mainly from the middle classes and was determined by their desire to maintain appearances by dressing to their position. The demand for cheap clothing was largely regulated by basic necessity. But in the post-War period, class distinctions in clothing have tended to disappear. Clothing purchases for many consumers, particularly those in the 15–30 age groups who now earn good wages in offices and factories, are no longer regulated by basic necessity. . . . Moreover, fashion now exerts a bigger influence on demand than before the war. Consumers in all income groups take a more general interest in fashion trends.[1]

In 1946 both consumer rationing and the Utility clothing scheme remained in operation. The Austerity period continued until 1949 when rationing was finally phased out, but Utility clothes remained in production and on the market until 1952. So while ostensibly little changed immediately after the War, consumers had become accustomed to quite good standards of price and quality in Utility clothes, despite the 'Make do and Mend' philosophy. The clothing industry had been forced to rationalise its operations and gradually saw the return of unrestricted supplies of fabric. The preoccupation with British couture design after the War probably stems from two related circumstances: one was the formation of the Incorporated Society of London Fashion Designers (Britain's answer to the Parisian Chambre Syndicale d'Haute Couture) and their involvement in the Utility scheme; and the second, a debate in fashion circles about whether London could ever become a world fashion centre. The two were linked because it was perceived that high style and design only resided in couture clothes (mass production inevitably copied and diluted their statements), and many commentators felt that a greater injection of 'design' — in terms of stylistic innovation — was needed in ready-to-wear clothing if it too was to improve its fashion reputation.

In 1942 the Board of Trade approached the Incorporated Society with a proposal that some of its members should co-operate in designing clothes for mass production. It was hoped that they would be hardwearing and simple in design but display the excellent cut, line and proportion for which British couture clothes had always been famed. All the designs were for retail sale and within Austerity specifications. British *Vogue* reported the collaboration and proclaimed it, 'a revolutionary scheme and a heartening thought. It is, in fact, an outstanding example of applied democracy.'[2]

It wasn't until just after the War that a more realistic appraisal of the scheme and its implications for the British fashion industry was made by one of the foremost writers on the subject, Alison Settle. Writing in *Picture Post* in 1945, she praised the Board of Trade's employment of couture designers under the Utility scheme but suggested that there were definite obstacles to London developing into a world fashion centre:

Success cannot come to English fashions so long as the men of the country treat fashion as being essentially frivolous and even laughable . . . to take the trends of fashion seriously, to discuss clothes seems unthinkable. Only when fashion trends, colours and the whole philosophy of clothes is talked about — as films, pictures and music are discussed — can the textile trades of Britain regain their merited superiority in the eyes of the world.'[3]

Alison Settle could not have foreseen the reputation of 'Swinging London' nearly 20 years later. It was a reputation that developed out of the work of a new generation of designers committed to high standards in the design of mass-produced clothes. Nevertheless, it was not until the 1950s were underway and the development of an 'affluent society' had begun that British fashion really began to stengthen and grow.

Great strides were made by clothing manufacturers and retailers in securing economies of scale; mass production and mass consumption together produced continuous growth. Large retail chains became increasingly common during the 1950s and their success was often achieved at the expense of independent provincial retailers. In a survey of the British fashion and textile industries in 1968 it was reported that,

> The growth of mail order houses and multiple stores selling their own branded goods (eg Marks & Spencer) has tended both to keep prices down, because of the aggressive buying policies they have been able to adopt, and to set standards of quality and manufacture, and reliability in delivery that the mass of smaller retailers was never able to achieve.[4]

Bon Marché haberdashery counter in Brixton, showing self-servic and counter service 1958 (Courtesy of John Lewis plc Archives)

Multiple retailing was obviously the natural adjunct to the growth of standardised large-scale production. Multiples such as Marks & Spencer, Littlewoods and British Home Stores planned their activites to secure economies in distribution costs and a reduction in purchasing costs by placing large production orders with manufacturers. The ownership of a number of retail branches brought these firms into direct contact with a considerable section of the market which helped them to make accurate estimates of current trends in tastes and prices. This was, and is, a vital part of sucessful fashion retailing; the ability to plan advance orders. Success, however, has usually been judged by these companies in terms of sales figures alone. Value for money and quality of manufacture has invariably taken precedence over the risks involved in design innovation.

The new high levels of turnover in fashion retailing achieved by the multiples did have an important influence on forms of garment display and shop interiors. In May 1952 *Design* magazine reported on 'New Settings for Selling Menswear' and asked,

> Is it too fanciful to see a connection between the development of self-service in food stores and the design of the latest Autin Reed shops? . . . though the customer cannot yet serve himself with menswear, in these shops the obstruction between him and the open displays of stock is reduced to a minimum.[5]

Developments in the retailing of foodstuffs and the emergence of large supermarket chains such as Tesco and Sainsburys had indeed begun to filter through into fashion retailing by the 1950s. Littlewoods, unlike Marks & Spencer, developed their branch stores along 'supermarket'

121

lines soon after the War, stocking a wide variety of food and household goods as well as clothing. Multiple fashion retailers aimed to utilise available floor space most efficiently with racks and rails of garments from which customers served themselves. It became clear that a far higher turnover of stock could be achieved with this kind of layout than by the established counter-and-aisle arrangement found in department stores and independent 'madam' shops. In 1957 *Design* magazine concluded that,

> The introduction since the war of self-service and self-selection methods of selling is having a far reaching effect on English shopping [but] . . . the rapid development of the self-service principle has outstripped the ability of most firms to find an adequate substitute for the personal and intimate character of traditional shops, a careful attention to design will become an increasingly important factor as competition grows.[6]

Design in this context meant the development of a 'house-style' or corporate image that would enable consumers to identify the companies and brands whose products they preferred. By the beginning of the 1960s competition had encouraged many firms and manufacturers to re-think their visual presentation. In terms of fashion retailers a house-style was particularly important for the multiple chain stores, where it helped to bridge a gap between the branches and, in department stores, to lend a unity to the merchandise as a whole. The concept of a corporate image became increasingly familiar in all areas of retailing and design during the 1960s — often peddled as indispensable by young design consultancies. For fashion retailers, however, it was a means of conveying the general image and market level of the company and creating an atmosphere conducive to the sale of merchandise. Increasingly it has also become a way of advertising and selling particular brands of taste and lifestyle, fashionableness, quality or value for money. For the multiple stores, suggesting value for money (without necessarily inferring a lack of quality) seems to have been the highest priority at all times. The justification for high pressure selling and a minimum of trimmings is usually that it is those very conditions which make it possible to offer the consumer such good value for money. Portraying an image of style or fashionableness has apparently been a secondary consideration for the multiples. Their conscious input of a design element was kept to the minimum necessary for successful trading in their chosen market. Even Marks & Spencer, who have a good reputation for quality and have encouraged higher standards among the multiples, place quality and value for money above style, fashion or design.

The main development in the field of department stores after the War lay in the success and expansion of a number of financially large trading groups. *The Economist*, in March 1955, reported that the Great

Universal Stores group had gained control of seven previously independent stores, and United Drapery Stores, nine. Other firms such as the John Lewis Partnership and Debenhams Ltd also controlled much larger groups of stores than before the War. However, few department stores (with the exception of the John Lewis Partnership) centralised their buying activities. This was almost entirely because, under strong competition from the multiples, individual stores had had to concentrate on supplying particular groups of consumers in their locality with good quality clothing. They could not compete in the market for high turnover sales of cheaper garments. The main advantage was a reputation for personal service and high quality merchandise.

It was through department stores that couture design found a more popular market during this period. Throughout the 1950s it was common practice to buy certain couture models — usually from French houses — and have copies made up for exclusive sale in the store. The John Lewis Partnership became involved in this type of scheme as early as 1950 when it formed a special collaboration with the Parisian Couturiers Associés. They obtained the exclusive right to copy, in their own fabrics, and sell the designs of Carven, Desses, Fath, Paquin and Piguet. A report in the *Gazette of the John Lewis Partnership* explained:

> Hitherto, English manufacturers have bought Paris models and copied and adapted them to sell over here, but this new idea is

123

unique inasmuch as the collection has been especially designed for production in this way. It is a concerted effort, a 'combined operation' to give a well balanced and comprehensive choice and every model will bear the original designer's name. . . . It is only by this fortunate arrangement which combines exclusive styling with comprehensive production, that the Partnership's customers will be able to indulge their appreciation of the design and beautiful materials at, in some examples, no more than Utility prices.[7]

For the couture houses this kind of collaboration became increasingly necessary for financial survival, and the decline of couture was not just an English problem. By the 1960s most fashion-conscious consumers were predominantly younger women whose interest in keeping up with the latest styles put greater emphasis on a high turnover of less expensive and, in design terms, less rigid clothes. Lack of demand and rising costs (for the production of couture clothing was highly labour intensive) forced many houses out of business. The greatest British survivors were Hardy Amies and Norman Hartnell, both of whom enjoyed royal and court circle patronage. But even they were forced to diversify their interests. Hartnell designed for Berkertex and subsequently became a consultant to Great Universal Stores, while Amies formed connections with Hepworth, Debenhams, Carrington Viyella and Vantona Textiles. The forging of links with manufacturing and retail organisations was recognised as the best guarantee of continued survival.

It is interesting that the event heralded as the start of a new fashion retailing revolution — the opening of 'Bazaar' on the King's Road by Mary Quant in 1955 — occurred only five years after Hardy Amies himself opened a 'ready-to-wear' boutique; the first, it is claimed, selling couture-designed 'off-the-peg' clothes. Judging by the now well documented success of the Quant organisation, real dissatisfaction with the products of mass retailers on the one hand, and exclusive stores on the other, did exist among enormous numbers of young consumers. According to Ken and Kate Baynes, writing in 1966, the boutique revolution had its origins

> deep in the larger revolution which has grown out of teenage affluence and the wider rejection of conventional values. . . . This new world of fashion is an entertainment world, inevitably linked with pop, and it reflects the same curious mixture of grass roots exuberance and big business success.[8]

The story of Mary Quant's business success is indeed astonishing: it is reported that during the first week of trading at Bazaar the shop took five times more money than expected, proving to its owners that,

> there was a real need for fashion accessories for young people chosen by people of their own age. The young are tired of wearing essentially the same as their mothers.'[9]

Facade of Mary Quant's Bazaar boutique in the Kings Road, 1966

Ten years later Quant was designing for 18 different manufacturers — including some in cosmetics and furnishings — and had licensing agreements around the world. In design terms the crunch had come when, acting as her own buyer, Quant failed to find existing merchandise that satisfied her taste. She came to the conclusion that Bazaar would have to be stocked with clothes designed (and initially made) by herself. The styles and shapes are now well known, but in the late 1950s they were highly innovative and attracted a huge market. What Mary Quant and other young designers of her generation succeeded in doing was to provide clothes for a young affluent market which they themselves represented. The clothes were certainly more expensive than typical chain store garments but they had a high fashion, individualistic design content and a feeling for contemporary young taste which was lacking in other available clothes in the same price bracket. It seems that, however enticing the teenage market was to the major manufacturers, fashion design specifically geared to them had not been taken seriously enough up to this point. Clothes from Bazaar and other similar boutiques were not necessarily cheap, but many young consumers had sufficient 'disposable' income and in any case the clothes were regarded as very desirable. Ken and Kate Baynes remarked of Mary Quant, John Stephen and John Michael — all of whom grew from tiny rented shops selling clothes they designed themselves to large retail organisations —

> It is clear that these three people were in touch with a need in fashion in the late 'fifties which completely eluded the larger manufacturers, and which was alive before anybody set about providing clothes which satisfied it.[10]

The fashion and boutique revolution started in the late 1950s continued to grow during the 60s fuelled by a second generation of designers, many of whom came out of the new art colleges, and pushed fashion specifically for the young market into the chain stores. Shops such as Etam, Martin Ford, Dorothy Perkins, Wallis and Miss Selfridge all blossomed during the 1960s and gave London a reputation for young fashion which it has never really lost. From the early 1970s, the Biba store in Kensington High Street is a consumate example of fashion design packaging which embraced a complete style of living. Part of the appeal was a nostaligia for past times of elegance and luxury, but there was also an element of individualism sought after by young consumers which suggests that once again the major retail outlets failed to provide sufficient choice or innovation in their products. A fashion for second-hand clothing developed in its own right, to which the success of the Flip organisation in the 1970s bears witness, as do indeed the hundreds of provincial second-hand clothing dealers that sprang up during the 1970s. They provided many young consumers — notably art students — with a source of individualistic clothes that are still regarded by many as superior, in terms of style, materials and manufacture than anything available from mainstream fashion retail outlets, and for a fraction of the cost.

Once again social changes have initiated changes in what is considered fashionable, and later fashion retailing itself. During the 1970s at least two waves of dissent against ideas of sartorial acceptability and 'a wider rejection of conventional values' were reflected in how young people in particular chose to dress: hippies and punks may have been worlds apart ideologically, but within roughly the same decade both groups adopted styles of clothing which were first regarded as extreme but which each constituted a new avant garde in fashion. 'Street

Interior of Flip, secondhand American clothing store in Covent Garden, 1980s (Courtesy of Malachite)

126

fashion' as it was dubbed, forced many fashion retailers to reassess their market and adopt a more flexible policy in terms of design. In turn, many manufacturers have had to come to terms with the risks of short production runs in an effort to keep pace with rapid changes in demand. Today many consumers rejoice in the multiplicity of fashionable styles, retail outlets and price levels which are more generally available. Indeed, since the 1960s, the market for fashion clothing has shown a strong tendency to separate into different and often distinct groups: the chain store multiples still attract a huge volume of business from more established consumer groups, particularly those involved in family buying. Marks & Spencer are fast becoming a chain of department stores. Clothes produced by a new generation of young designer–makers are highly influential in the international fashion world and attract large numbers of consumers and copyists — as Katherine Hamnett found to her cost. The chains of shops catering for essentially teenage consumers specialise in a very high turnover of fashion styles each season, and couture design (again with the bonus of royal patronage) is attracting sufficient numbers of wealthy consumers to flourish again. This wide range of retail sources for fashionable clothing seems to demonstrate that many smaller independent organisations are successfully providing what the large, centralised multiples could not do alone, and that the exhibition of individual taste in clothing has become a fashion in its own right.

REFERENCES

1. Margaret Wray *The Women's Outerwear Industry*, Gerald Duckworth, 1957, p 58.
2. Unattributed, 'Fashionable Intelligence' in British *Vogue* March 1942, pp. 25–31.
3. Alison Settle 'London: Can it Become a World Fashion Center?' *Picture Post*, January 6, 1945.
4. Caroline Miles *Lancashire Textiles: A Case Study of Industrial Change*, Cambridge University Press, 1968, p 95.
5. 'New Settings for Selling Menswear' *Design* No 41, May, 1952, pp 24–7.
6. Alec Heath 'New Ways with Selling' *Design* No. 103, July, 1957, p31.
7. *Gazette of the John Lewis Partnership* 'Paris Models for the Modern Pocket' 21 October 1950, p443.
8. Ken & Kate Baynes 'Behind the Scenes' *Design* No. 212, Sept 1960.
9. Mary Quant quoted by Barbara Bernard in '*Fashion in the 60s*' Academy, 1978.
10. Baynes. Op cit.
11. Alastair Best 'Shops', *Design* No.300, December, 1973, p38.

THE FURNITURE RETAILER AS TASTE-MAKER
PENNY SPARKE

In the never-ending discussion about the state of modern furniture, which invariably focuses on the 'failure' of British design and the execrable taste of the British public, one important element is usually missing: seldom is the role of the furniture retailer even mentioned, let alone analysed in any depth. In an attempt both to fill this gap and to confront yet again the question of why Britain is so far behind the Italians, the Scandinavians and the Germans in its capacity for good modern furniture design, I would like to consider the significant role that retailing has played, since the end of the Second World War, in influencing both the production and the consumption of modern furniture.

The period which begins with the Britain Can Make It exhibition up until the present day is a long one, and many fundamental changes have taken place within both patterns of consumption and British manufacturing. The first important change, where retailing is concerned, was the expansion of mass consumption which began in the second half of the 1950s and continued through the period. The social historian, Arthur Marwick, calls 1957, 'the first year of the new consumer society'[1] and it is around this same time that the disparity between the ideals of the British 'good design' propagandists and the taste of the mass of the British public was highlighted for the first time. Through its increased spending power, the mass market now posed an open threat to the programme of design reform which the Council of Industrial Design had initiated in the aftermath of the Second World War. Where furniture was concerned, the disparity manifested itself most clearly in the difference between the pieces illustrated in the Council's publications and those displayed in the shop windows of the high street furniture retailers. The latter were blamed for perverting the tastes of their new 'uneducated' customers and for exerting pressure on manufacturers to produce what they maintained the public wanted.

Before going into the details of the crisis of taste in British furniture in the late 1950s, in which the retailer was so firmly implicated, I shall first consider, briefly, the dominant patterns of furniture retailing in the period leading up to that date.

In the 1930s, well over 90% of household furniture went through retailers in Britain and their influence was already being felt by manufacturers who were producing numerous goods specifically for them.

128

As Dr Suzette Worden has pointed out in her thesis on British furniture in this period,[2] the wider availability of hire purchase emphasised the retailers' tendency to put pressure on the manufacturer to produce increasingly cheap furniture with a growing emphasis on novelty for novelty's sake. In 1938 at least 60% of furniture was sold on hire purchase terms but, while this was common sales practice for the new multiple furniture stores which were appearing in suburban and provincial high streets all over Britain, it was less evident in the way department stores and the specialist furniture stores handled their business in this period. Traditionally, since the second half of the 19th century, the department stores — among them, in the 1930s, Harrods, Schoolbreds, Selfridges, Whiteleys, Barkers and Oetzmanns — and the specialist shops — among them Heals and Dunns of Bromley — had provided furniture for the middle-class market: they continued, and still continue, to perform this role in the period after the Second World War. Their pre-eminence was, however, already on the decline and, by the 1950s, they had become relegated to the fringes of furniture retailing in Britain. Conversely, as J B Jefferys points out in his book *Retail Trading in Britain 1850–1950*[3], while in 1939 multiples accounted for between 15 and 17% of total furniture sales, by 1950 this had already expanded to between 19 and 23%. The proportion was to move swiftly upwards in the following decade.

Shop window from 1957 showing hire purchase facilities

So far as the nature of the goods sold by the multiples was concerned, there was also a strong sense of continuity through from the 1930s into the 1950s in the retailers' and, consequently, in the public's, preference for suites of furniture, whether for the living room, the dining room or the bedroom. This can be explained simply by the fact that, for the retailer, suites represented a marvellous selling advantage: they looked more impressive in the showrooms than isolated furniture pieces and, seen from the window, enticed the new customer into the shop. Also, with the problem of obtaining sufficient turnover associated with payments through hire purchase, the sale of suites enabled larger sums of money to flow through the business and keep it more buoyant.

While the pre-War period saw the beginnings of a development which was to continue logically into the 1950s and to reach a head at the end of that decade, the War constituted a temporary hiatus. It seemed to some people at the time as if it was in fact going to bring about a permanent change of attitude in the taste of the mass of the British public. The idealism of Gordon Russell and his team focused on the hope that the simple aesthetic of the Utility furniture would bring about reform in that area. He wrote optimistically that, 'I am one of those who believe that this grading up may well be permanent.'[4] Freed from the bonds of Austerity, it wasn't long before the public was clamouring once again for the bulky three-piece suites that it had coveted in the pre-War years. Russell's words sound naive in retrospect.

Furniture shop window from 195 showing emphasis on suites

Where retailers were concerned, the Utility scheme — the production of a limited number of furniture pieces made to standardised designs and available only to the most needy through a coupon system — meant that they could only obtain new designs against the units they got from their customers. Thus their stock was limited and they had nothing to display in their windows. Their fall back position was to depend increasingly upon second-hand goods and antiques.

The effects of Austerity lasted well into the early 1950s. From 1945 up until then the furniture trade, both from a manufacturing and a retailing point of view, made brave efforts to re-establish itself: it became increasingly evident, however, that the lessons of Utility had not penetrated far into British society. The shortage of materials, particularly wood, meant that new furniture was in limited supply, although a number of experiments with metal indicated that new ways were being found to manufacture much-needed furniture items. At Britain Can Make It, for instance, Ernest Race exhibited a dining chair made of aluminium, and Heal and Son Ltd displayed its metal garden furniture designed under the directorship of Christopher Heal. These innovations were not widely available, however, and in general terms the post-War years saw a reversion to traditional, repro-traditional and antique furniture retailed through the department stores and specialist shops which catered for the top end of the British market. Where the rest of society was concerned it was simply a case of making do or of buying on the second-hand market.

A wide range of better grade Dining Sets from 45½ Gns. or 9/- weekly

Advertisement for reproduction furniture from the 1950s

4' 6' Sideboard with Illuminated Cocktail Compartment. Flush Top Draw Leaf Table. Upholstered Back Chairs. £68-12-6 or 13/3 weekly.

The high-class, London-based producer–retailers — among them Heals, Dunns, Bowmans and Storys — and the department stores — including Arding & Hobbs, Liberty, Harrods, Oetzmanns, Whiteleys, and Harvey Nichols — remained supreme in this period, offering Utility furniture alongside second-hand and antique furniture to the 'discriminating consumer'. In 1947, for instance, Harrods claimed that it offered 'the quality, charm and dignity of a bygone age'[5] to customers in its furnishing galleries. By the end of the decade 'period' and 'modern' co-existed in the showrooms of all these outlets and gradually, as restrictions were lifted, these stores began to experiment with 'Contemporary' furniture, a new style which combined essentially 18th century details, like tapered legs and winged backs on chairs, with new materials and production techniques.

The main enthusiasm for Contemporary came from the CoID which encouraged the new generation of designers, emerging from the War, and a number of small, progressive furniture manufacturers (among them Ernest Race, Hille and Archie Shine) to identify with their campaign aimed at raising standards in British furniture design and turning Britain into a competitor on the world market. Where retailing was concerned, all the stores listed above had, by the early 1950s, incorporated a Contemporary setting into their showrooms and many of them, particularly Heals and Storys, went as far as instigating the design and production of Contemporary pieces, the first under the supervision of Christopher Heal and the latter by Ian Henderson.

By the middle of the decade it had become apparent that the imbalance of supply and demand which applied ten years earlier had completely reversed itself: as a result both of the generally increasing affluence of the period and the expansion of new housing — most of it centred in provincial 'new towns' or in estates outside city centres — demand now outstripped supply. In addition the popularisation of the Contemporary style, achieved by the Festival of Britain had created a demand for new furniture in the modern idiom rather than for reproduction pieces.

The trade was quick to respond to this, and the retailers in particular played an important part in establishing the nature of the pieces that the new customers were to take into their homes. This was largely in the hands of the high street multiples and the mail-order companies which had taken their businesses into the provinces and the suburbs and which adopted an aggressive sales policy. As in the 1930s, most payments were made by hire purchase and credit arrangements: this was often isolated as the key factor in the 'watering-down of taste values', as the design reformers of the day saw it, that was occurring in the mass consumption of furniture in this period. According to the CoID, the official taste makers of the day, the new consumers sought glossy, superficially impressive qualities in their purchases and were ignorant about the subtler features of modern furniture designed according to the criteria of good craftsmanship and visual discrimination. Writing in the *Ideal Home Yearbook* of 1955, for instance, Paul Reilly, soon to be director of the CoID, complained bitterly about, 'the sort of half-baked, eye-catching misrepresentations of originally good ideas that are everywhere coming to the fore in the gaudier windows of the cheap furniture emporia.'[6]

These sentiments quickly turned into a general battle cry, as the public was exhorted to 'think before you buy'. The gap between the high street chain stores, which stuffed their windows full of glossy, bulbous furniture pieces, all offered at competitive prices on reasonable terms, and the more up-market department store or specialist shops which displayed contemporary pieces in spacious room settings was absolute and seemingly unbridgeable. The roots of this dichotomy were both social and geographical and its irreconcilable systems of values were clearly manifested in the pages of volumes such as the *Ideal Home Yearbook*. Here in 1953–4, for instance, an advertisement for a lumpy, 1930s-style settee-bed could be seen directly opposite an article by Gordon Russell illustrated with Council of Industrial Design-approved Contemporary furniture with elegant tapered legs. In the article he described what he saw as the main problem that, 'there are towns where not a glimmer of the ferment which is going on today can be discovered.'[7] He regretted deeply that 'flashy and meretricious goods often appear to give an impression of luxury and costliness to the ignorant when seen from the pavement and skilfully lighted.'[8]

The emphasis was well and truly on the retailer, seen as the evil manipulator of working-class taste, the reason behind the manufacturer's tendency to cheapen and distort his products, and the essentially conservative force behind British design. The same argument has often been repeated since the late 1950s and is used as the explanation for the preponderance, in the 1960s, 70s and even the 80s, of bad-quality, 'teak-finish' furniture available in high streets all over Britain. The arbiter of taste, in this context, is seen to be the buyer or salesman who knows what sells, or rather what has sold in the past, and manages to persuade (by dint of making nothing else available), his customer to buy what he has to offer. The customers, already entering into the 'disrespectable' practice of buying through a hire purchase scheme, seek respectability and status in their furniture and therefore buy what their neighbours, or family, bought before them. It is an argument which tends towards circularity and to suggest that the only solution is education on a mass scale — a solution frequently put forward by the CoID (but without, it must be added, much success).

An alternative contemporary account of working-class furniture purchasing in Britain in the late 1950s is provided by Richard Hoggart in his book *The Uses of Literacy*. Unlike the design reformers, Hoggart is less concerned to condemn the tastelessness of high street furniture than to understand the nature of its appeal to the working-class consumer. He concludes that the customers are persuaded to buy the furniture by the friendly, personal manner of the salesman who goes

'Furnishing Today' exhibition held at Rowntrees in Scarborough, sponsored by the CoID, 1951

out of his way to make his customers feel at home, and writes, 'This is a consistent and powerful use of the individual and domestic approach and all the nicer because unexpected in so posh a gentleman'.[9] The customers, he suggests, are lured by a feeling of intimacy and security and are attracted by the smartness of the salesman who offers, in addition to the glitter of the furniture, 'a suggestion of education and elegance.'[10] It is an argument which suggests an extreme gullibility on the part of the working-class consumer.

So far as the design reformers were concerned, the geographical and social differences in styles of furniture retailing and patterns of consumption in the late 1950s led to an impasse. However, developments within society as a whole and (as a direct response) within retailing itself, resulted in the emergence of a possible alternative to the established relationships between the mass furniture retailer and the mass market. While department stores and specialist stores continued to provide 'tasteful' objects for an 'educated' market, and the generation of mass consumers outside London who had become accustomed to the high street chain store continued to depend on its 'teak-finish' products, a new style of furniture retailing emerged in the mid 1960s which was influenced by the new rash of 'fashion boutiques' aiming to provide individualistic, brightly coloured, visually stimulating goods for the young and affluent.

The 'retail revolution' of the early and mid 1960s coincided with the realisation that the atmosphere in which you buy something is as important in influencing your purchasing decisions (especially where 'lifestyle' goods are concerned) as are the nature and price of the product purchased. There was a yawning gap between the department stores or those exclusive shops which traditionally sold 'status' and 'quality' at a price to the top end of the market, and the high street chain store which sold on price and stylistic acceptability and ignored quality and presentation. Added to this was the emergence of a new youth market — many of them newly married — who were wealthier and more independent than ever before, with a high disposable income for lifestyle and fashion accompaniments.

The other stumbling block for traditional furniture retailing had been the problem of delivery time which became longer and longer as manufacturing became increasingly mass-production oriented and, as a result, less flexible. Consumers wanted instant gratification from their purchases and were less willing to wait for their newly acquired goods. One manufacturer even wrote apologetically in an advertisement in 1964, 'Please be patient with our delivery. Craftsmanship cannot be rushed.'[11]

One response of furniture manufacturers to the loss of faith in retailers, which resulted from the drabness of their stores and the inefficiency of their service, was to bypass them and to sell direct from the factory with the use of catalogues. Numerous advertisements in popular home magazines of the early 1960s exhorted customers to visit their showrooms and buy direct.

Where the fashion trade was concerned all these factors combined to favour entrepreneurs like Mary Quant and John Stephens who introduced the concept of the 'boutique' in which 'shopping became an entertainment, not an ordeal'. A little later, but with exactly the same aims in mind, Terence Conran opened his first 'Habitat' store in the Fulham Road in 1964.

The fundamental class division reflected in and catered for by British furniture retailing was not broken down overnight by the new approach, as has sometimes been suggested. The small 'design-conscious' furniture boutiques that emerged in the mid 1960s — among them 'Anderson Manson' in the Fulham road and Zeev Aram's austere little shop in Covent Garden, and even stores like 'Trend Interiors' in Richmond — were never aimed at the high street market and Conran's first shop was no exception to this rule. They remained avant garde and expensive. But as Arthur Marwick has remarked in his book *British Society Since 1945*, 'the new (youth) culture was much more widely diffused than any other avant garde culture has ever been.'[12] This was particularly true in the area of fashion where ideas were quickly picked up and reproduced for the mass market. By the late 1960s, it had become increasingly true of furniture also. In many ways age rather than class alone seemed to be the major social divide in this period.

As a result of the emphasis on youth one significant change in furniture retailing in this period was the inclusion of furniture and furnishings with other products for the new lifestyle. Thus a shop like 'Gear' in Carnaby Street — Mecca to many adherents of the new youth culture — sold old pine chests painted in psychedelic colours by Binder, Vaughan and Edwards alongside second-hand military clothes and Union Jack washing up cloths. The new emphasis on furniture as part of the general Pop environment forced new modes of retailing upon it and allowed new furniture styles to penetrate new markets. Shops like 'Goods and Chattels' in Neal street and the 'Merchant Chandlers' in the Fulham Road, for instance, sold stripped pine chests with brass handles alongside feather dusters and soap. Owned by the fashion photographer Terence Donovan, the latter shop was modelled on Conran's original Habitat store which stocked a whole range of lifestyle goods from pots and pans to wicker baskets and candles.

By the mid 1960s the first signs of stylistic eclecticism and revivalism had become established as a firm element within the repertory of styles offered to the new style-conscious youth market. It existed alongside the 'knock-down' and 'throwaway' designs that grew out of the Pop movement and which, from a retailing point of view, circumvented the problems of delivery, thereby turning furniture, like fashion, into a form of instant gratification.

The most significant innovations that Terence Conran injected into furniture retailing in Britain (apart from introducing the idea of self-service which had moved from food retailing into fashion before coming into this area), was the idea of selling a whole domestic package to the consumer that was co-ordinated by a single eye. He had trained and worked as a furniture designer in the 1950s and was acutely conscious of the problem of selling new, exciting furniture through traditional retailing outlets. He complained bitterly about the preponderance of teak and brown moquette in British furniture which had become inextricably linked with the high street furniture chain store and he established Habitat in 1964 as a means of selling domestic items that he would consider buying for his own home. Habitat sold instant pre-packaged 'good taste' rather than furniture and therefore the appearance of the shop environment was of paramount importance. Conran developed a simple interior aesthetic both for the store itself and for the homes for which his products were destined, which was characterised by plain whitewashed walls, natural floors and a mixture of well positioned objects, both old and new. The shop gave an impression of spaciousness which contrasted dramatically with the overstuffed, claustrophobic atmosphere of the high street stores, and the brightly coloured goods he had carefully selected were shown seductively beneath spotlights.

The huge success of the first Habitat store led to inevitable expansion and, by 1968, there were four Habitat retail shops in Britain. The Manchester store, for instance, was opened in 1967 and had an identical house-style with white paintwork, quarry tiles, an open stairwell and a high degree of visibility from the street. A commentator in *Design*

137

magazine wrote at the time that 'Habitat should add to Manchester's lively image now that there is the new "village" area, off Deansgate, with its boutiques, cafes and discotheques'[13] thereby clearly allying Habitat's customers with the young market that had emerged in that decade. Habitat was beginning to compete openly with the provincial furniture shops by this time and to provide a mass-market alternative to the multiple stores that had dominated the trade in the 1950s. Price was still important but the policy of importing cheaper foreign goods and of concentrating on flat-packed knock-down furniture which facilitated storage and distribution were the ways of keeping costs down rather than relying on shoddily made 'safe' furniture to guarantee sales. Inevitably Habitat appealed to a young, fairly affluent market and it quickly became a force within British furniture retailing in this period: in 1968, for instance, the shops had a two million pound turnover.

While many of the small furniture boutiques established in the 1960s had come to a sticky end by the end of the decade, Habitat went on expanding and by 1974 there were 18 stores in Britain. Many furniture specialists and high street stores lost their pre-eminence at this time and had to rework their images as a result. The Perrings chain of family shops based in the south of England, for instance, which had survived competition from national chain stores and furnishing boutiques, felt the need to revive its house-style in 1967. It was an essentially conservative store, dependent upon customers who had been coming to it for a long time, and was well aware that it, 'cannot move too fast without running the risk of frightening away regular customers'.[14] It limited its face-lift to the use of new lettering for its facia and to putting a new emphasis on co-ordinating an interior: a carpet display in the Croydon store, for instance, showed how important it was to co-ordinate that particular furnishing element. The new Perrings store in Kingston was designed as part of the new Civic Centre and showed, in its sense of internal space and the emphasis on the new role of lighting in its displays, a clear debt to the Habitat style of marketing furniture and furnishings.

Facade of John Perring furnishing outlet from 1963

138

By the early 1970s Habitat had lost its exclusive image of a decade earlier and become a familiar sight in many provincial towns. Unlike the furniture chain stores of the 1950s which were integrated into the ribbon high street developments of the inter-War period, it was found in renovated areas, particularly the new pedestrian precincts of the late 1960s. These offered consumers a new retailing experience: multi-storey car parks allowed them to drive away their newly purchased, flat-packed storage systems and the experience of acquiring instant packaged 'good taste' replaced, for many young consumers, the earlier practice of signing a hire purchase agreement and waiting for their new dining-suite to be delivered when the retailer could get it from the manufacturer. Credit cards speeded the whole process up and Habitat's control over its manufacturers increased delivery efficiency.

For those young people for whom Habitat was too expensive, second-hand furniture was still the only alternative and the fashion-ability of Victoriana and 'stripped pine' in the late 1960s and early 70s encouraged a sudden renewal of interest in slow-down furniture shops. This can be directly linked with the slow-down of building in this period and the consequent interest in renovating Victorian town houses. Habitat was also quick to jump on the band-wagon, introducing repro-duction Victorian furniture and other domestic items. Stylistic eclecti-cism and constant innovation became the store's main marketing policy — a complete reversal of the essentially conservative stance of the high street stores.

In an article about Terence Conran, written in the late 1970s, Stephen Bayley wrote that, 'Instead of replacing the high street furni-ture retailing giants, Habitat has joined them.'[15] This was true on one level only: while customers could, inevitably, still only buy what was available to them, those goods had been pre-selected, not simply on their price and qualities of instant appeal but on the basis of a set of 'taste-values' which they both manifested and openly propagated. Habitat was no less manipulative than the retailers it superseded — in fact the subtlety of its marketing policies made it all the more persuasive in wooing customers into its premises and controlling the manufacturers who provided its products. The difference was in the visual nature of those goods and in the concept of taste that lay behind their selection. As a taste-maker Habitat was pre-eminent, but its concept of taste was pre-formed rather than established solely by the habits and aspirations of its customers: it was a formula which, inevitably, many copied, but none with equal success.

In spite of the unmitigated success of the Habitat policy of selling 'good taste' to an increasingly visually aware young market at a price it could afford, the established forms of retailing didn't vanish overnight. Many, like Perrings, simply revamped their image and carried on with renewed energies: the department stores built on their reputations for quality, continuing, through this period, to take advantage of the more avant-garde experiments and to import 'designer-furniture' from abroad. Woollands in Knightsbridge, for instance, exhibited some of the most interesting and experimental of the Pop pieces at its exhibition 'The Breakthrough Designers' in 1965 and both Harrods and Liberty imported 'chic' Italian furniture and sold it alongside more traditional items. The more exclusive specialist shops, which had by now established a tradition of a dealing in modern design — among them Oscar Woollens, Zeev Aram and Heals — also consolidated their position of providing expensive modern furniture for a specialist market at this time.

Therefore, at the top and middle of the market, 'good taste' was well catered for, mostly by pieces designed and/or produced abroad (usually Italy, although still to a certain extent Scandinavia) and also by Habitat and its numerous branches. Where the bottom end of the British market was concerned, however, there were, by the early 1970s, signs of an emerging crisis, created both by the recession in the British furniture manufacturing industry (which had traditionally provided the high street chain store with the bulk of its products) and by the growing competition of the 'democratization of taste' brought about by progressive retailing. The trade's solution was to repeat the formula of the 1950s: to think solely in terms of price and established consumer preferences.

What emerged was the concept of the 'furniture warehouse', among them Harris Queensway, Vogue Interiors and MFI. Based on the American retailing idea of taking customers out of town to large sites with low overheads, the warehouses provided not only more choice than the high street chain store, but also more generous credit facilities. There was no attempt to provide packaged 'good taste' in the Habitat sense but instead a range of stylistic possibilities was on offer. Today, for instance, in a Queensway store the customer can choose from stripped pine, Danish teak, country cottage style, 'Habitat' bright colours, 'modern' chrome and glass, mahogany traditional etc. The idea is to provide a selection of current styles, whether modern or traditional, in the hopes of meeting all possible customer preferences. The furniture is all mass-produced and priced for the bottom end of the market: all the models are in stock and many of them can be carried away in flat packs. Most of it is specially made for Queensway by British manufacturers, large concerns which are not economically geared to take risks. As in the 1950s and for exactly the same reason, there is at Queensway a special emphasis on the suite of furniture.

A sense of stylistic anarchy pervades the interior of these retailing outlets and the display is very basic. There is no attempt to create the ambiance provided by Habitat and there is a strong implication that the 'no frills' approach is consistent with the lowest possible prices. Credit buying is the most dominant form of purchasing here and Queensway, for example, makes customers aware when they enter the

140

store of its budget account scheme which offers them up to £1000 of instant credit.

In 1969 a writer in *Design* magazine commented that, 'the colourful visual revolution has only touched the surface of the massive teak mausoleum.'[16] Ten years later this was still true as the furniture warehouse made abundantly obvious. One of the reasons was that British manufacturers shrank in number by half between 1959 and 1969 and thereby became dominated by giant, automated firms which were unable to take the same design risks that their smaller, more flexible, Italian counterparts were, and are, so adept at doing. The furniture retailer, also, plays a crucial role in determining the nature of their production.

In the 1980s the gap between the up-market, London-based, or more specifically, Covent Garden-based 'design-conscious' furniture retailers importing chic Italian products or selling fashionable items to a young wealthy market and the provincial high street chain store or furniture warehouse is as great, if not greater, than the one that existed in the 1950s between the department stores and the high street multiples. In spite of the so-called 'retailing' and 'taste' revolutions that occurred in the 1960s and the apparent bridging of the social gap that is supposed to have taken place in that decade, the situation in the 1980s shows little change from 30 years earlier. The continued gap reflects the entrenched nature of the class system within British society, a system which is reinforced by the nature of the developments in public and private housing programmes since the War. Inevitably, also, it is reflected in styles of retailing and patterns of consumption. Arthur Marwick describes the continuation of the British class system, 'The forms of class are deeply entrenched in British society; they were not seriously challenged in the Forties, when they might have been, and were only slightly modified in the Sixties.'[17]

The question of taste is clearly as much a sociological as an aesthetic problem. Class differences are the basis of the marketing decisions which determine the nature of the furniture that retailers supply. This market-led approach towards retailing will never lead to a renewed attitude towards 'taste-making' or, by implication, to a shift in the social structure. The lesson from the 1960s is that, although people can only buy what is made available to them, they (or the younger ones among them) are as likely to buy furniture which has been selected for them on a taste basis as on a price basis, provided that it is offered at a price they can realistically afford.

The central question then arises of, whose taste is being, or should be, sold? Is it the taste of the projected customer or that of the retailer? Habitat showed that, with a designer in charge, it was possible for a retailer to project his taste on to his customers and to achieve a positive response. The argument often put forward to counter that suggestion, however, is that once it hit the high street, in the early 1970s, Habitat began to reflect, rather than to determine, public taste which was being disseminated by the mass media. The other counter argument to the viability of the Habitat approach is based on a distrust of the imposition of taste values from one class to another, which was an inevitable result of its manner of retailing.

The parallel of the 1950s and the 1980s is, however, an illuminating one. It indicates that, in spite of the recent advances made in Britain in popularising the concept of design — advances that resemble very closely those achieved in the 1950s by the design propagandists of the day — there is a strong sense of 'preaching to the converted' going on today. Also, until the complex concept of taste and its disseminators are examined at all social levels, the dualism that Paul Reilly isolated back in the 1950s, whereby 'good design' is immediately 'debased' by its contact with the mass market, will continue to dominate the production and sales of consumer goods in this country. In this exercise the role of the retailer, who is, after all, the agent who decides what the public will buy, will need to come under careful scrutiny.

REFERENCES

1. Marwick A *British Society Since 1945*, Penguin, 1984, p18.
2. Worden S *Furniture for the Living Room: An Investigation of the Interaction between Society, Industry and Design in Britain from 1919-1939* PhD thesis (unpublished), Brighton Polytechnic 1980.
3. Jefferys J B *Retailing in Britain 1850-1950* 1954, p428.
4. Russell G 'Furniture' in *Design 46* Council of Industrial Design, London 1946, p94.
5. An advertisement for Harrods Furniture in *Ideal Home Magazine*, 1947.
6. Reilly P 'Look Before You Buy' in *Ideal Home Yearbook* 1955, p62.
7. Russell G in 'How to buy Furniture' in *Ideal Home Yearbook* 1953/4, p59.
8. Ibid
9. Hoggart R *The Uses of Literacy* Penguin, 1957, p108.
10. Ibid p107.
11. An advertisement for 'Strongbow' furniture in *Ideal Home Magazine*, 1964.
12. Op cit 1 p129.
13. Gray I 'Habitat Shop for the North' in *Design*, Nov 1967, p30.
14. Meade D 'Perrings at the Crossroads' in *Design*, Nov 1967, p55.
15. Bayley S 'Mr. Habitat' in *Architectural Review*, 1978, p289.
16. Duckett M 'New Furniture' in *Design*, Feb 1969, p49.
17. Op Cit 1 p218.

Part 6

Design and the Public

Part Six looks at the way that the general public has responded to the attempts made in the years after 1946 to raise the standard of its taste. It is a thorny question which puts much of the work of the design reformers, the design theorists and many designers themselves into a critical perspective. The first essay, written by Lucy Bullivant, a historian of modern design who graduated from the Royal College of Art in 1984, examines the response of the public to the Britain Can Make It exhibition itself. Catherine McDermott, a lecturer in the history of modern design at Kingston Polytechnic, takes the 1950s as a case study decade for a discussion of the ideological gap between design reform and public taste in this country.

As the other sections have indicated, this is one of the key issues in an assessment of British design since 1946, and there is much more work (primarily of a sociological nature) to be done concerning the nature of taste and consumption patterns. Only with a thorough understanding of these difficult concepts will design reformers of the future be able to make any significant headway.

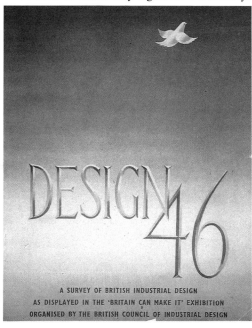

A SURVEY OF BRITISH INDUSTRIAL DESIGN
AS DISPLAYED IN THE 'BRITAIN CAN MAKE IT' EXHIBITION
ORGANISED BY THE BRITISH COUNCIL OF INDUSTRIAL DESIGN

Cover of Design 46, *the book that accompanied the 1946 exhibition*

'DESIGN FOR BETTER LIVING' AND THE PUBLIC RESPONSE TO BRITAIN CAN MAKE IT

Lucy Bullivant

Britain Can Make It was formally launched in 1944 amid some criticism that it was premature in view of Britain's new production phase and shortage of staff and materials. However the venture was justified by other influential parties within the design establishment precisely on that basis, and a special grant of £240 000 was given to the Council of Industrial Design by the Board of Trade. This move was a 'well-calculated act of national policy',[1] because it was felt that the exhibition would promote a number of important issues: the lessons to be learnt from American industrial design techniques; the increased role played by design consultants; and the notion that good mass-produced design was crucial for economic prosperity and an improved standard of living.

The debate as to whether the exhibition should have been held reflected a complex ideological dilemma: the issue being that what contributed to a state of progression in domestic architecture, furnishing and decoration could equally well create a state of retrogression. Britain was pictured as facing a threat to her overseas trade. The threat to our balance of payments and the threat of war should be wholly different,

*King George VI and Queen Elizabeth
opening Britain Can Make It in 1946
(Courtesy of The Topical Press Agency)*

but in the rhetoric of propaganda the two tend to be equated for the purpose of combatting their effects. It was necessary to break down in people's minds the memory that Britain had been a nation at war, and to build up a sense of active transition from destruction to creation — the beating of 'swords into ploughshares'.[2]

Britain Can Make It had three overlapping intentions. The first was to present a shop window showing Britain's ability to compete on the international market. Britain emerged from the Second World War as a debtor nation tied to complicated land lease agreements and, stripped of many of her foreign investments, badly needing to boost her level of exports. To make matters worse, a manufacturing revolution had taken place in the USA during the previous 15 years, making many of Britain's exports appear old fashioned. The design of machine-made goods thereby assumed a new importance: 50% more exports were needed to get back to pre-War levels, which had been around £400 million, at least half of which was contributed by industries whose sales were greatly affected by design.[3] Apart from this export target, Sir Hugh Dalton, President of the Board of Trade (from February 1942) also wanted to capture a large home market. The dollar export drive launched by Sir Stafford Cripps in the late 1940s created an overwhelming national need to prevent a drain on dollar resources. Policies such as the imposition of customs duty on imported films had a far-reaching effect upon Britain's cultural life, restricting information about America and nurturing a shell of insularity. Official propaganda put forward ostensibly clear-cut arguments in which aesthetic criteria did not feature: 'Britain must earn her keep. We cannot buy anything we cannot pay for'. But elsewhere a double-edged stress was placed upon competition, one which was simultaneously economic and aesthetic: asserting the need to promote a positive national self-image of a country able to adapt to modern techniques, and compete with America. Britain Can Make It was the British government's search for a national style which was not modernistic or gimmicky but rather based upon Britain's past reputation.

Noting the impact of international competition on the prosperity of the home market, the editors of *The Studio* sagely remarked in their 1948 *Yearbook* that,

when trade is bad the design of industrial articles often shows improvement. Manufacturers are more willing to seek new designs during a depression, as a stimulus to the public, than when there is a seller's market, and they are too busy producing to think of experimenting with new design.[4]

However the CoID regarded the design policy of many firms and manufacturers as one which had not changed since before the War. Their approach was negative — to avoid market hazards — and led to their being highly cautious of innovative or artistic endeavours.

The second declared aim behind Britain Can Make It was therefore to show British manufacturers that 'good design' was good business, and that high standards could be made 'to serve the ends of commerce'.[5] This involved breaking down the established idea that industrial design was 'something beautiful and remote, high-minded and a little uncomfortable.'[6]

To the public at large, the exhibition was intended to demonstrate the importance of 'design for a rising standard of living',[7] providing in the words of Paul Reilly, a 'crammer's course in the practical problems of design.'[8] The emphasis was on the exhibition as an educational exercise, promoting a package of practical and utilitarian standards behind which was an assumption that complete design control offered a chance to impose 'good design' upon a supposedly passive, receptive public, in the same way that Utility furniture had been imposed as a result of the material shortages of the War.

S C Leslie, the first Director of the CoID, wrote optimistically in *The Times* of 4 October 1946 of a

> contracted bad taste market, subjected to the combined effect of the BBC, the Arts Council, the discussion group movement and world travel in the services.[9]

He was evidently referring to part of the general public comprising the Council's audience, the 'leadership group'[10] identified at the Council's inception. This initial market research further distinguished a second larger group of adults — 'the uninterested' — some of whom could be wooed by connecting images of dress with domestic furnishing wherever possible in broadcasting and women's magazines.[11]

The third main aim of the exhibition was propagandistic. Britain Can Make It was undoubtedly a conscious attempt to direct and dictate taste by encouraging a movement away from pure utility and towards some degree of strictly controlled decoration with an arts and crafts rather than an industrial base.

However, the newly formed CoID failed to anticipate the reaction of the exhibition-going public and, although the general response was positive, it did not have the thoroughgoing educative effect its organisers desired. Instead the public, as the results of an independent survey (discussed later) show, revealed itself as possessing a discriminating spectrum of attitudes, but as being united in its demand for access to a wide range of consumer goods. This demand could not be met under the stringent rationing regulations and most of the articles in the exhibition had labels on them indicating an approximate date from which they would become generally available. Transferral to peacetime entailed prolonged shortages of goods for the following ten years. As a matter of political expediency, the government introduced in 1948/9 a 'bonfire of controls'[12] on the distribution of a variety of industrial products.

The exhibition itself involved assembling 20 selection committees for each of its sections. Some 3 385 manufacturers contacted the CoID with details of over 15 000 articles from which 5 259 products were selected to be shown, chosen from 1 300 different exhibitors. It was stressed that space was not sold, and the machinery of selection used independent judges, advisory committees and technical assessors. The combined experience of the 70–80 designers employed to work on the various sections spanned exhibitions from Wembley (1924) to New York (1939–40). The whole of the ground floor of the Victoria and Albert Museum was made available for the exhibition which occupied about 90 000 square feet, and boasted a fixed circulation route of one-third of a mile.

An independent, and unique, survey of the exhibition was commissioned from the Mass Observation organisation. This was set up in 1937 by the anthropologists Tom Harrison and Charles Madge (then a journalist on the *Daily Mirror*) as an independent, fact-finding body, documenting the processes of social change, of political trends, and public and political opinion in a series of books, bulletins and broadcasts. Between 1937 and 1947 they undertook the largest investi-gation into popular culture in Britain this century, motivated by the need for 'an anthropology of our people'. It became clear from their study of 'real life, mass circularised images and "fictions" from news-reels and events' that there was a gap between what ordinary people thought and what the press, media and political leaders said they thought.[13]

Mass Observation's organisers regarded their survey of Britain Can Make It as a major one in terms of work undertaken, involving 2 523 interviews, and its findings assume a greater importance still as the only serious piece of market research which retrieved and recorded consumer attitudes towards design produced in the early 1940s. Public reaction to didactic exhibitions about design was not gauged further by the Council, beyond an investigative excursion into responses to the Design and Industries Association exhibition 'Register Your Choice',[14] mounted at Charing Cross Underground station in 1953.

The furnished rooms section of Britain Can Make It, 'Things in their home setting' (designed and co-ordinated by the architect F R S Yorke), together with 'Shopwindow Street' (designed by James Gardner) were deemed to be the most popular sections (almost one in four visitors mentioned the room set section as the one they liked best after seeing the whole exhibition). Of the 24 rooms arranged on either side of a narrow passageway and carefully designed around a specific 'role model' family grouping, the one which found the most favour with the public was a cottage kitchen designated 'working-class utility' (designed by Edna Mosely). This belonged to a miner and his family and, like all the other room sets, was accompanied by a cartoon by Nicolas Bentley illustrating the occupants in a characteristic group.

Comments noted revolved around how removed from reality the set room was in terms of space allowed. Mass Observation's own comment was that it was,

difficult to have a taste for anything other than neatness and unobtrusiveness in homes which are too crowded and probably poorly designed.[15]

Spectators commented on the necessity of better designed housing before focusing attention on the aesthetic presentation of interiors. The omission of a kitchen table from the room did not go unnoticed by the public, particularly as the kitchen was traditionally the centre of domestic life in working-class homes.

It was intended that the role of design as part of daily life should be emphasised, not as something to be admired from a distance. However from the most modestly fitted to the most lavish, the model kitchens presented were laid out like film sets, and the survey showed that people responded towards them as showrooms, and assumed the role of detached spectators, without direct engagement. In the four kitchens shown the stress was on better labour-saving machinery. In the other rooms, as the social scale ascended, personalised objects such as photographs of film stars, plants, telephones and book shelves were introduced, together with a greater subtlety in colour schemes and greater use of pattern (for instance Edward Bawden's designer wallpaper in F R S Yorke's 'middle-class living room'. For the affluent homes framed works of art were shown on the walls (by Yeats, Pasmore and Christopher Wood) which, according to the Mass Observation survey, were universally disliked. This was attributed to the fact that they were, 'rather ahead of and less related to public taste than any other item on show.'[16] What was not clear was whether the rooms were intended to show what the Council saw as the existing make-up of social class structure in ascending groups, or role models for the future.

The reception to the furniture on show depended upon whether it was Utility, non-Utility or the half-way 'Diversity' range. According to the survey, the public roundly rejected anything that was part of a Utility range, but retained a taste for simplicity but not plainness, especially in ceramics. Also, whilst being preoccupied with newness, it did not endorse 'futuristic' design in particularly large numbers. Clive Latimer's birch and aluminium cabinet for Heal's was criticised by one member of the public as looking 'too much like a fridge'. Although visitors wanted to see objects which functioned efficiently (but without necessarily supporting the Council's avowed dictum 'Fitness for purpose'), greatest interest was aroused by objects such as R D Russell's radio cabinet built into the wall of the barrister's 'luxury living room'. Antique furniture was in evidence but only in one luxury room because although 'repro' was considered by the organisers anathema in any situation, the original Adam gilt table *was* deemed appropriate in a wealthy setting.

Antipathy to plastic goods was common, for they bore the stigma of 'cheapness' and 'commonness'. China (then still in short supply) was a much more sought-after material and, reasoned one individual,

> the advantage of china over plastic is that you get more variety of colour — you don't get the pastel shades in plastic.[17]

Cost did not dominate people's reactions. Within the glassware section people favoured the more delicate styles; again the presence of plainer, Utility styles in the exhibition was not welcomed. Their ubiquity and forced standardisation throughout the five years of Utility had earned them a reputation for flimsiness and poor quality. Mass Observation noted, 'a strong desire amongst almost everybody to have in their ideal home what they had seen in the course of their visit.'[18] The artefacts were regarded as pieces in an artificial juxtaposition, and few spectators appeared to consider the rooms as concepts which could be instantly applied, even partially. Few commented upon the 'case histories' devised and displayed above each room.

As a public assembly of ostensibly new, designed products the exhibits in Britain Can Make It did not successfully compare with their American and German equivalents in the late 1930s, although ironically Gardner and Spence's exhibition design itself *did*, featuring the familiar amoeboid form throughout. It was said of the designers that,

> to the geometric forms associated with contemporary architecture they have joined ornamentation in a different idiom.[19]

With a few exceptions, the industrial artefacts within this dynamic framework, from textiles to teapots, were derivative of pre-War designs, reflecting the sluggishness pervading a market in which few genuinely new designs were being put into production, and for which no new retail outlets or shop refurbishments had been provided since 1939. The display in 'From War to Peace' (a set designed by Beverley Pick) of a new type of saucepan — its improved nature the result of a manufacturing process itself informed by research on the durability of Spitfire exhausts — indicated that war could bring technological advancement through the innovation of necessity, but conveyed its message with a mundane product, not enhanced by its juxtaposition with other examples such as waterproof fabrics, laminated plywood, cigarette boxes and high-heeled shoes.

Didactic statements about taste were framed within 'Shopwindow Street', a group of brightly lit shop windows, the backdrop of which was a dark blue sky with the faint afterglow of sunset, flanked by decorative murals by Duncan Grant, Vanessa Bell and William Crosbie. The set utilised Surrealist motifs such as the disembodied hand and, in its treatment of individual objects such as domestic utensils, showed a move towards the 'opening up' of shops pioneered by American designers. British designers in the 1950s either discarded the fully enclosed window with its mahogany back, or pierced it to allow for at least a partial look into the shop itself. The fully cased display of selected items of merchandise remained for the large store, but then the tendency was to enlarge the entrance and make the transition from pavement to sales counter as 'casual' as possible.

Within other transitional sections, such as two showing an early 20th century kitchen scene (which, again, were packed with appliances), the techniques of contemporary retail display were eclipsed in ingenuity by the use of semi-reliefs and distorted perspective. The placing of the objects chosen — vacuum cleaners, breadbins, kettles and kitchen curtains — and the addition of drawings representing others had none of the didactic approach of the earlier sections but followed instead an aesthetic approach intended to be viewed as a whole.

'Shopwindow Street' offered opportunities for user participation in the form of the 'Quiz Bank' produced by the Design Research Unit. This dispensed plastic coins for the 'shopper' approaching the scene to use to give his or her vote of confidence for one of three comparative

'War to Peace' section of Britain Can Make It, designed by Beverley Pick

151

Display of antiquated kitchen equipment, designed by J Bainbridge

designs of objects, amongst them armchairs, lampshades, gas fires and teapots, which were presented in 12 pictorial groups in the accompanying *Design Quiz* publication. It was pointed out by the organisers that the images were not meant to represent objects which were considered very bad, medium and very good designs, as the text asserted 'even the experts do not always agree entirely.'[20] However the possibility of dispute seemed negligible given the 'truth to materials' advice:

> . . . always reject a design which imitates something else; electric fires which imitate coal fires, wood which imitates marble; inexpensive things which try to look rich by wearing a lot of fancy decoration, just as we all dislike showy people.[21]

Of the visitors who made their selection, in seven out of twelve cases there was a variance from the public and the experts, the reason being that in most cases, while the experts had evidently placed function as their prime criterion, those participating rejected the utilitarian option on aesthetic grounds, particularly when considering crockery, glassware and the three radios on display. That the experts advised that a radio should look like a radio, and not an imitation of something else, seems to have influenced people hardly at all. The results confirmed the opinion of the Mass Observation group that, 'the general public is much more critical and analytical of the goods that are displayed in shop windows than is generally supposed.'[22]

'What Industrial Design Means', devised by Misha Black, Bronek Katz, R Vaughan and Austin Fraser, presented an apparently neutral, explanatory picture of the machine, representing the technology of mass-produced domestic artefacts. On the face of it, the display raised many fundamental points but in fact explained a few superficially, ignoring crucial areas of the design process involved in the production of, in this case, egg cups. At the entrance stood three cardboard caricatures — two sturdy ones representing figures of the design establishment, and the third a spindly, 'average' member of the public, pointing the way into the section as they 'converse' via speech balloons:

'Take a good look. Think over what you see and judge for yourself.'
'Will I find good design here?'
'These questions will put you on the way to good design.'

A plastic press, described as making 3 000 egg cups a day, was reported by Mass Observation as being the centre of interest of this section, one reason being that it was a working model, as opposed to a static object. In general, explanatory text was kept to a minimum, the exhibits 'being allowed to speak for themselves.'[23] The intention was to encapsulate the 'doctrines' of the previous sections, and give the visitor

the means of judging, with increased understanding of the role of the designer in the manufacturing process, the examples of good design which are displayed elsewhere.[24]

However, whilst the importance of the idea of the designer as hero in the grand scheme was stressed, there was no clear comment on how industry functions, no historical background on particular industries, no explanation of the reasons behind manufacturers' choice of products, and no attempt to define the potential and possible future development of mass production. The importance of design to manufacturers, the role of design as part of a process involving market research, product development, marketing and advertising, was nowhere discussed and was evidently felt to be beyond the scope of the exhibition, and the grasp of the visitors. These omissions were out of step with the Council's intention to,

help to rehabilitate as a family a series of displaced persons, forced apart and scattered by the industrial revolution — maker, salesman, teacher, artist or designer, retailer, user.[25]

As a result, notions of the operations of the marketplace and the making of judgements about taste appeared to have little connection with one another. However, what did undoubtedly emerge from 'What Industrial Design Means' was a sense of Britain beginning to respond to the challenge set up by the USA, particularly through the emerging role of the consultant designer.

Apart from the general irritation expressed about the non-availability of most of the objects on display, other adverse comments about the exhibition centred on its lack of originality (controlled decoration), the essentially pre-War designs, and the fact that 'the propaganda was bigger than the exhibition'. There were a few accusations of favouritism from manufacturers; from display staff of some retail companies, some condemnation of the exhibition designers' use of 'high art', particularly in the display of new materials and Shopwindow Street: 'a bad Surrealism . . . the Bloomsbury corduroy school is in power.'[26]

Mass Observation's analysis and implicit criticism of the Council's propaganda about design was clear in its publication *Change*.[27] This centred around the idea that the origins of MO lay in the efforts of the Ministry of Information's exhibitions promoting themes such as salvage or gas masks, many of which failed to connect with public feeling. Success in putting a message across and securing public interest was, however, gained through a breakaway from the formal pattern, and the mounting of special sets, models, machines and demonstrations. Britain Can Make It represented an effort to achieve this, but the Council's inadequate grounding and background research restricted its effectiveness. Detailed field studies by Mass Observation during the War revealed a considerable misunderstanding of the public mood by the government,[27] such as the underestimation of support for mass conscription of woman power, or the lack of official awareness of potentially influential areas of mass propaganda such as dance music.

The public response to the Council of Industrial Design's first major exhibition revealed that there was in essence a fundamental discrepancy between the Council's assessment of its audience (ie a largely undifferentiated, two-tier social system of middle and working class) and Mass Observation's perception (a three-tier system containing numerous internal variations). According to Mass Observation's survey the most widely represented class at Britain Can Make It was very definitely artisan working class.

Viewed as a thematic forerunner to the Festival of Britain, for which the idea of design as an intrinsic part of civilisation was developed, Britain Can Make It presented design as an indivisible moral concept to be applied to society using the terminology of what was most practical, most fitting for its purpose. In spite of the exhibition design, the tone adopted conveyed a wartime ideology of unity and uniformity. In the 1940s, from the point of view of the Board of Trade, what ultimately had to be communicated by the CoID was that design was important for a rising standard of living; demand had to be nurtured to meet the needs of production.

In 1946 Sir Thomas Barlow had envisaged that, with the inception of a future design centre, the Council would be able to

> dig below the surface of the market and report on the trends of public need, often before the public itself is clearly aware of them.[28]

Its inability to do this was in large part due to an inadequate definition of post-War social relations and their role in developing Britain's industrial base.

REFERENCES

1. Council of Industrial Design, *2nd Annual Report: 1946–7*, HMSO, 1947, p 4.
2. Sir Stafford Cripps, Foreword, *Design '46*, survey of British industrial design displayed at 'Britain Can Make It', 1946, ed. WH Newman, Council of Industrial Design, 1946.
3. Sir Hugh Dalton, *Design '46*, ibid.
4. *The Studio Yearbook: Decorative Art 1943–48*, 1948.
5. Sir Thomas Barlow, CoID *2nd annual report: 1946–7*, op cit.
6. Ibid.
7. Sir Stafford Cripps, foreword, 'Britain Can Make It', *Supplement to the Board of Trade Journal*, 28 September 1946, p 1.
8. Paul Reilly, 'Industrial Design in Britain', *Stile Industria*, February 1956.
9. Leslie, S C 'Britain Can Make It: overseas buyers' interest in exhibition', *The Times*, 4 October 1946.
10. Council of Industrial Design, *First Annual Report 1945–46*, 1946.
11. Ibid.
12. Imposed by Harold Wilson, President of the Board of Trade, March 1949.
13. Mass Observation quote from 'Mass Observation: the Intellectual Climate', David Mellor, *Camerawork*, 11 September 1978.
14. Mass Observation report, *Design and Industries Association Yearbook*, 1953, pp 15–23.
15. Mass Observation, *'Britain Can Make It': B. Effects of the Exhibition: Taste, Design and Consumer habits*, 1946, unpublished manuscript.
16. Ibid.
17. Ibid.
18. Ibid.
19. Raymond Mortimer, 'Britain Can Make It!', *New Statesman and Nation*, 28 September 1946.
20. *Design Quiz*, Council of Industrial Design, 1946.
21. Council of Industrial Design, *First Annual Report 1945–46*, 1946.
22. Mass Observation report, op cit.
23. Misha Black, *Exhibition Design*, Architectural Press, London, 1950.
24. *Supplement to the Board of Trade Journal*, op cit, p 14.
25. S C Leslie, 'Britain Can Make It', op cit.
26. Stafford Bourne, 'Britain Can Make It', *Display*, April 1947.
27. *Change*, bulletin of the Advertising Services Guild. No. 2 'Home Propaganda', 1942, prepared by Mass Observation; no. 4, 'People's Homes', 4th national survey sponsored by ASG, March 1943.
28. Sir Thomas Barlow, CoID *2nd Annual Report: 1946–47*, op cit.

POPULAR TASTE AND THE CAMPAIGN FOR CONTEMPORARY DESIGN IN THE 1950s
Catherine McDermott

A glance through design magazines of the 1980s reveals a witty, idiosyncratic 'interior image' of our times. One sees illustrations which stress the slightly precious, individual taste of the avant garde, showing exclusive interiors and creative experiments which challenge the nature of conventional mass production and which mark a shift of interest away from popular taste. Against a visual backdrop of Post-Modernist decoration and colour, the feeling is of hard times and individual success. These attitudes have turned the focus of design inwards. Discussion about design ethics or social problems is usually met with a wry smile. The implication is that the problems of professional survival are enough. In this respect contemporary design has placed itself in a neutral position which mirrors the more general lack of confidence in our cultural priorities and their future.

This is, then, an appropriate moment to look back to the 1950s when design had a much more positive role to play. This chapter looks at the optimism and social concerns that preoccupied post-War Britain, and at the campaign, promoted by the Council of Industrial Design and the design profession, to make design accessible to all social groups. It is not easy to make the imaginative leap between the commitment to social idealism in design that characterised that period, and the cynicism and élitism associated with the 1980s. It is impossible, for example, to imagine a modern equivalent to the 1956 exhibition at the Whitechapel Art Gallery, 'Setting Up Home'.[1] The catalogue, sponsored by the department store in Bethnal Green, Oxford House, was an open letter to Bill and Betty — a mythical working-class East End couple — suggesting ways in which a budget of £50 could be spent on contemporary furniture. It would be a brave exhibition that proposed ways in which the new generation of low-paid workers and unemployed might benefit from the advantages of a 'designed' environment. For holders of a UB40, the Department of Health and Social Security allows furniture grants which enable access only to the most dismal second-hand markets.

In the 1950s the idea, however naive, that design was democratic was widely accepted. 'Today decent furniture is within anyone's reach. For the first time in a lifetime we are nearing a classless style. Contemporary furniture and textiles look just as well in a council flat as in a West End flat, just as well in a City office as in a Chelsea studio.

Retailers who have pioneered these new ideas have reported that people of all classes are their customers, bus drivers, bank clerks, school teachers, artists, doctors and company directors alike.' Paul Reilly, respected figure in the design establishment and Director of the Conran Foundation, made those comments in 1953, in an article called 'Don't Be Afraid Of Contemporary Design'.[2]

What exactly did Reilly mean by the term 'Contemporary'? The CoID was usually careful to couch any definition in generalised terms: 'the Council's propaganda has always been towards encouraging fresh thought and design in both the old craft-based and the new technical industries, whether the inspiration for a good design is original and contemporary or basically traditional.'[3] The same kind of reply was given by Gordon Russell to a salesman at a Council conference on furniture, who asked him outright, 'What is good design?': 'Design is constantly evolving and it is not possible to give definite rules.'[4]

In visual terms we now recognise Contemporary as a style which used bright primary colours, new materials and techniques, sculptural and often quirky shapes, in small-scale flexible furniture systems. In ideological terms, Contemporary implied a commitment to design values which promoted modern consumer products not exclusive on grounds of cost. In this way Contemporary design was, in theory at least, part of the movement of radical social change affecting post-War Britain. The politician, Rab Butler, evoked the spirit of the period when he wrote in 1960, 'We have developed an affluent, open and democratic society in which the class escalators are continually moving and in which people are divided not so much between the "haves" and "haves nots" but between the "haves" and the "have mores".' Reilly's

Interior of house in Hampstead 1954 showing contemporary furnishing

comments that Contemporary design was equally available to the bus driver and the doctor were part of the same belief that the War had brought about fundamental changes to democratise Britain. These same changes were pinpointed by the social critic Richard Hoggart, in the opening paragraphs of his seminal book *The Uses Of Literacy*, 'It is often said that there are no working classes in Britain now, that a "bloodless revolution" has taken place which so reduced social differences that most of us inhabit an almost flat plain, the plain of the lower-to-middle-classes.'[5] Hoggart was reporting received opinion rather than fact. In contrast, George Orwell's perception of social change did not include a belief that class divisions were disappearing. What he did concede, however, was that certain experiences contributed to a general levelling effect; he wrote, 'Ready-made clothing, for example, made it harder especially in the case of women to determine social status at a glance. Mass-produced literature and amusements had the same effect.'[6]

Design, it was hoped, would also have the same 'levelling' effect. The precedent for this was the Utility scheme, of which the purpose, in Gordon Russell's words, was 'to raise the whole standard of furniture for the mass of people.' One of the shared beliefs of post-War design thinking, upheld by members of the CoID and associated groups, was that, in theory at least, everyone could participate in design and there was a general commitment to the concept. These viewpoints were, admittedly, made more feasible by full employment and the expanding economy of the 1950s but they were the beliefs held by the most influential sections of the design profession, and were disseminated through articles, lectures and personal appearances on radio and television.[7] In this respect, Robin Day was typical of his generation when he described the Contemporary style, which he pioneered in his furniture designs for Hille, as 'the concept of enlightened good design'. In this sense Contemporary design became part of the mood of national pride, the sense of common experience and purpose, and the commitment to rebuilding post-War Britain.

What, in this context, were the strategies used by the CoID to democratise design? The key to its policy was education and it was Gordon Russell who became most closely identified with this programme: design education was something with which he had been spiritually and temperamentally in tune since the 1920s. He had absorbed the Arts and Crafts values of his youth and later took much interest in the model of Scandinavian design, with its basis in democratic socialism. In practice, however, the CoID's plans to raise the quality of ordinary life through design had a strong middle-class appeal. In 1947, in collaboration with Penguin, it produced a series of slim hardback books called *The Things We See*, each one selling at 3s 6d. The best known title was *Furniture* by Russell but others included Misha Black's *Shop Windows* and Ashley Havinden's *Advertising*. An indication of their intended audience can be drawn from the cover which stated that the intention of the series was to 'direct the eye and mind to a cultured discrimination'. Another scheme introduced Council-approved Contemporary design into a decidely middle-class preserve, the department store. And *Design* magazine reviewed a Council-sponsored exhibition at Elliston and Cavell in Oxford in 1956, which was part of a whole series of events including displays of Contemporary furniture, design literature and public lectures.[8]

Show house at Hatfield new town, 1953, with CoID-approved furniture

Interior of Robin and Lucienne Day's home in Chelsea from the early 1950s showing contemporary furnishings

A much wider audience was reached through magazines. Hoggart noted in 1957 that, 'newer and glossier magazines are capturing the working class audience' and Hulton readership figures support his view.[9] In 1938 *Woman* magazine had a circulation of 75 000: by 1957 it had increased to 3 500 000 and was read by half the female population aged between 16 and 44. The CoID looked very carefully at ways in which it could use these magazines as, during the 1940s, the government had used them for official information. In 1948 Aneurin Bevin called a press conference for women editors asking them to run a feature on the Labour reform bills, and the CoID took over this role by sending a number of magazines ideas for joint projects, which could be converted into suitable articles. In 1952 Mary Grieve, then editor of *Woman* magazine, was invited to sit on the CoID's committee, which at that time included Geoffrey Dunn and Robin Darwin among its members. In her autobiography *Millions Made My Story*,[10] Grieve recalled the role magazines played at that time in discussing the Contemporary style,

> The fact that bulbous, veneered and over-ornamented furniture of 30 years ago is practically gone from the shops in favour of clean lines and pleasanter woods, is partly because the millions of new small homes built over the last 15 years would just not take the massive stuff. But public acceptance of the new look was slower than it was in dress. The home editors of the women's magazines have helped the furniture trade enormously by their consistent demonstration of the post-War look in furniture.

Woman assigned feature writer Edith Blair to cover design. At first her articles had a typical wartime flavour; a simple feature from 1 January 1949 was headed *Painting Old Furniture in Modern Colours*. Gradually, however, numerous articles appeared dealing with the novel problem of buying new furniture but slanted towards those who were operating on a low budget. This stress on ordinary family requirements remained a consistent feature of magazine policy in the early 1950s. On 28 May 1949, a story called 'Here's the story of how Dick and Diana furnished their new council flat' showed how Dick, a shop assistant on £6 10s per week, was given a budget of £200 to select simple unit furniture. Social problems were also discussed. 'Bill and Muriel set-up home' helped a couple, living with their in-laws, choose Contemporary furniture for their two rooms. In 1952 *Woman* ran a feature on John and Betty Surlees, in their brand new council house in Peterlee, surrounded by CoID-approved design. The lighting, by Troughton and Young, was accompanied by Kandya chairs, Hilleplan units, Race seating and dhurry rugs. Articles like these in women's magazines virtually repeated the Council's Design Index and were careful to provide information about pricing. A free booklet called *The Sitting Room* given away with *Woman* on 7 March 1953 gave advice on how to budget for an entire room. The cost of a Robin Day tele-chair?

Around five pounds depending on fabric. What is interesting is that exactly the same furniture was appearing simultaneously in more up-market magazines like *Homes and Garden*, although simple line drawings and black and white photographs were replaced by glossy colour spreads and more details about individual designers and stockists.

The CoID certainly intended that the message of Contemporary style should reach the widest possible audience, and as well as magazines, they looked to television. By 1959, 95% of the population had access to a television, and the BBC actively supported the Council's Design Index. It used, for example, approved lists to furnish sets for contemporary drama and, in 1953, 'Joan Gilbert's Diary' was the first chat show to use Contemporary design; viewers saw guests interviewed on Hille seating units and Race Festival chairs, while programmes like 'Come Dancing' used the chair Robin Day designed for the Festival Hall for its panel seating.

The set for the fortnightly TV programme 'Joan Gilbert's Diary' which commenced in 1953

Set for 'Come Dancing' (Courtesy of BBC TV Archives)

A major question that has to be asked is, persistent and worthy though the campaign for the democratisation of Contemporary design was, did it actually affect working-class lives? The decade produced little serious consumer research. In 1945, on the initiative of the Council and the Board of Trade, the Central Office of Information published a social survey report on furniture.[12] Its brief was to explore the issue of taste, particularly 'modern simplicity versus old-fashioned decoration' but the conclusions were vague: 'housewives in the lower income groups like the modern styles less than those in the higher income groups.' More in-depth studies such as Dennis Chapman's *The Home and Social Status* (1953) included data on the types, amount and arrangement of furniture in working-class and middle-class homes but did not deal with the issue of style and taste. Such evidence as does exist supports the view that Contemporary furniture was not bought by a working-class market.

By the late 1950s those firms pioneering cheap, mass-produced contemporary furniture had dropped out of the market. Hille, for example, ditched their innovative Hilleplan range in favour of the more lucrative contract market. Sir John Perring, then buyer for the family retail chain of the same name, recalled that the actual amount of Contemporary furniture sold was very small. At a Design and Industry Association conference in 1950, a buyer from a West End London store reported circulating a questionnaire asking reps to report on the trend towards Contemporary design: 'three-quarters reported no trend and the remainder that the increase was due to the middle and upper middle classes.'[14] Neither is there any evidence to suggest that the actual quality of modern furniture design available to a working-class market was much improved from pre-War years. Hoggart scathingly called it 'chain-store modernismus, all bad veneer and sprayed-on varnish.'[15]

The idea that the economic divide between rich and poor substantially narrowed in the 1950s was undoubtedly a mythical one. Although spending on domestic articles had increased by 115% during the period 1951–61, it was not evenly distributed over all the social classes. By 1964, for example, only 15% of social category DE (those earning £700 per annum) owned a fridge.[16] When working-class teenagers achieved relative affluence in the 1950s, their spending patterns suggested allegiance to a totally different set of cultural values than those promoted by the establishment.[17] Vivienne Nicholson, the wife of a Yorkshire coalminer who won the Football pools, recalled her priorities in her autobiography *Spend, Spend, Spend*; hair dyed Pink Champagne blond to match a new Chevrolet Impala, a holiday in Las Vegas and a Spanish-style bungalow in Garforth called The Ponderosa.

Having looked at some of the ways the CoID promoted the Contemporary style, and the inevitable difficulties it faced, I would now like to consider more precisely what role designers played in the early 1950s.

Would it be fair, for example, to describe designers during this period as a group of dedicated social reformers?

In the immediate post-War period designers did not enjoy a high status. In fact the reality of their position was often desperate, as Michael Farr's 1953 *Survey of British Industry* suggests, 'In provincial towns designers are often cooped up year after year in ill-lit inadequate studios at the beck and call of the sales manager.' In order to make a contribution to the post-War regeneration of British industry, designers needed to re-define their role and status. In this sense their commitment to Contemporary design included at least an element of professional advancement. Not irrelevant in this context is an off-the-cuff comment from the managing director of John Lewis at a Council conference in 1953 that, 'the Contemporary movement is the best sales promotion that the furniture trade has had for 50 years.'[18]

But the early 1950s was a very creative period for the emerging design profession. Designers began, for instance, publishing articles and books defending their position. In 1946, John Gloag wrote *The Missing Technician in Industrial Production* in which he set out to describe the situation of British design consultancy services at this time. His most interesting case study was the Design Research Unit, the first large-scale design consultancy in Britain, set up by Misha Black and Milner Gray. Both designers had an important impact on design attitudes in the 1950s; Black was a practical and humane man and virtually the only British designer to achieve an international reputation, while Milner Gray's book *The Design Profession* set out the ground rules for a code of professional practice for the designer. Both men saw education as the way forward, particularly the new design departments set up by Robin Darwin at the Royal College of Art. Ironically it was these two institutions, the CoID and the Royal College that reflected the worst aspects of the design profession at this time — its fundamentally closed shop, establishment nature, which was almost exclusively male and middle class. Writing in the mid 50s Robin Darwin said,

> We know you won't get good designs from the sort of person who is content to occupy a small back room. A man who won't mix because his interests are too narrow to allow him to, a man who is prepared and by the same token, only deserves to eat, as it were, in the servants' hall.

It is hard now not to wince at such blatant snobbery, but Darwin was right in one sense — the design profession must be seen to argue and debate current thinking and future directions.

With the benefit of hindsight we can say that the values and social conditions on which the campaign to promote contemporary design (a mixture of patriotism, economic growth and confidence in Britain's future), have now disappeared. The CoID's aim to make 'good design' accessible to all levels of society was valid but it could not claim any serious success in the mass market. The needs of the working-class community were never seriously explored and the essentially middle-class aspirations of Contemporary design were ultimately rejected. However, a more serious accusation that can be levelled at the design profession in the 1950s is the naive assumption that Contemporary design was something people should actually *want*. In their defence, the designers who promoted the style at least allowed a wider discussion of the social implications of design, however inadequate their analyses of it. In the 1980s this kind of critical evaluation from designers is virtually non-existent.

REFERENCES

1. Setting up Home, *Art and Industry*, 1956, p 101.
2. Reilly, Paul 'Don't Be Afraid of Contemporary Design', *Ideal Home Annual*, 1953.
3. Council of Industrial Design, *Annual Report*, 1953.
4. *Furniture*, typescript report of a conference organised by the Council of Industrial Design, 1949.
5. Hoggart, Richard *The Uses of Literacy*, Pelican, 1957, p 13.
6. Orwell, George, *The Collected Essays, Journals and Letters*, Vol 2, 1940–3, Secker and Warburg, p 77.
7. See, for example, *Design is Your Business*, a BBC television programme in which Robin Day and Gordon Russell discuss 'the best and worst taste in British design'. Reviewed in *The Cabinet-Maker*, July 1956, p 131.
8. Stewart, Jean, Courses For Customers, *Design* 86, 1956, p 24. Stewart, Mary *Experiment in Newcastle, Design* 1958 pp 27–8.
9. Hulton readership data is compiled annually by Research Services.
10. Grieve, Mary *Millions Made My Story*, 1964, p 93.
11. Meade, D, Furnishing The New Towns, *Design* 98, 1957, p 42–6.
12. *Social Survey Report: Furniture*, Central Office of Information, 1945.
13. Chapman, Dennis *The Home and Social Status*, Routledge Kegan Paul, 1955.
14. See report headed 'Contemporary Designs, Are They Really Popular: Conflicting Views?' *The Cabinet Maker*, 18 November, 1950, p 636.
15. Hoggart, p 31.
16. Corley, T A B *Domestic Electrical Appliances*, Cape, 1966, p 17.
17. See Abrams, Mark *The Teenage Consumer*, London Press Exchange, 1959. A short report analysing working-class teenage taste and spending patterns.
18. Typescript of a Council conference on *Furniture* held on 29 October, 1953, p 43.

Conclusion

It is hard to know where to begin in summing up the issues that have been raised in this critical survey of British design since 1946. One thing is clear though; it is meaningless to try and analyse one aspect of this complex web of themes involved without looking at its dependence on the other aspects and the way it interrelates with them. It is, for instance, impossible to think about manufacturing without referring to retailing and the consumer as well, and unwise to consider the achievements of the Design Council without looking at its influence across a broad social spectrum. The critic of recent design needs the skills of a social, economic, cultural and political historian in order to be able to place it in a context which makes sense: it's clearly not a task to be taken on lightly.

Well, Did Britain Make It? The answer is, of course, both yes and no. If we compare ourselves with Japan, Germany and Italy — all of them advanced manufacturing countries deeply committed to the role that design plays within production and sales (however differently they interpret the concept) — we are clearly not in the same league. Few of our products have any 'design clout' on the world market and our contribution there lies more with the traditional goods that we have to offer than with innovatory products. The reasons for this are complex: they are linked, historically, with the fact that we industrialised early in the traditional, craft-based industries; with our relative late entry into the so-called 'technological industries'; and with our emulation, in the latter area, of the American model of mass production without an understanding of the dramatically different nature of our home market. Thus we are stuck with a high-volume industry in many areas (such as furniture or electronics) that lacks the flexibility of both its Japanese counterparts, (which make great use of subcontraction to smaller component companies) and Italian manufacturing industry (which operates on a flexible, small-scale, high quality basis). This is a thesis which has been expounded at length elsewhere, but the period since 1946 serves to show how, in the recent past, this inflexible, mass-production approach has led to problems. Add to this the fact, excellently elucidated by Martin Weiner in his recent book on the cultural implications of British industrialisation that, in spite of its early entry into the world of large-scale industry and mechanisation, Britain has never become emotionally and culturally suited to this way of organising its production.

There are, inevitably, other reasons for the relatively low profile that design has had within British goods over the past 40 years: many of them have been touched on in this book. They include our late realisation of the importance of marketing; a general lack of communication within manufacturing industry between the art-trained designer, the science-trained engineer, and the business-trained manager; the relative low status of the designer within British industry; the dependence of industry, and perhaps more significantly the retailer, upon the perceived tastes of the mass market (and the reluctance, on both their parts, to innovate or lead the market); our insistence on selling on the basis of price rather than design; the lack of public knowledge of, and confidence in, the benefits of good design; the sociological naivety, or indifference, of the various design promotion bodies; and finally, the general suspicion, in this country, of the role of creativity in business and everyday life.

Together these criticisms add up to a fairly uncomplimentary and damning picture of the role of design within British post-War society and culture.

There are, fortunately, a few pluses to consider as well. We should not, for example, underestimate the way that the changes within British society in the late 1950s and early 60s forced open the whole debate about design and culture and projected new social and cultural meanings for the designed artefact. We should not forget also that in the 1940s and 50s the social message of design was very clear and that there was a sizeable group of highly creative, articulate British designers who were committed to changing society through design. The work of the CoID in that decade, however naively conceived it may seem in retrospect, was also full of highly laudable ideas.

Our innovations in designer-led retailing, from Habitat in the 1960s to today's smaller Covent Garden shops, are also important breakthroughs in this period and suggest that we are not simply prepared to let the law of the high street take over. The other, parallel development which deserves mention here is the recent expansion of designer-led, small-scale manufacturing concerns which also have their roots in similar experiments of the 1960s. There is a feeling emerging that, if nothing can be done to resuscitate the dead body of large-scale manufacturing in this country, the alternative way forward is for designers to organise the small-scale manufacture of their own products. This has grown noticeably in the past few years and is largely the result of art-school-trained designers realising that there is no place for them within the traditional structure of British industry.

The corollary of the common complaint that 'all our best designers leave this country and go and work abroad' is that they very often come back after a couple of years and apply their newly acquired experiences and confidence to improving the state of British design. Many of them set out on their own in the areas of fashion, textiles, furniture and products and show that objects can be produced by batch- as well as by mass-production techniques.

The role of art education in producing young, highly creative British designers should not be underestimated either. It is, in many ways, the most positive development, where design is concerned, of the post-1946 period and it is these young designers who will determine the future of design in this country. Linked to the concept of student design is the role of Britain's so-called 'street culture' in influencing international fashion and style. It has done so, in fact, since the 1960s when 'Swinging London' first became this country's major export. (Many of the young pop stars of the day were themselves products of the art schools.) While we may not be selling colour televisions on the world market we are certainly exporting 'youth culture' — fashion, graphics and fashion-related products — to a huge number of countries.

The role of the British design consultancy has also been touched on in the pages of this book. The development of a highly professional, flexible and internationally acknowledged and used consultant design service is another of the positive trends to have emerged in the period since 1946: it suggests that design skills should be considered as a service industry in its own right rather than simply as a back-up for our manufacturing industries.

Finally I return to the vital question of the public's response to design. There are indications, with the amount of mass media time and money now dedicated to the subject, that there is a desire to communicate the meaning and importance of design to a mass audience. The speed of communications has accelerated enormously since 1946 and the structure of British society, although not radically altered, has at least been shaken up. Ideas move more quickly than ever before from one sector of society to another. Also, ideas about design travel along different routes through society today — it is no longer simply a case of the Council of Industrial Design dictating the terms about the nature of 'good design'. Design is, in 1986, a much more open-ended, pluralistic concept than it was in 1946, expressing, simultaneously, a number of different meanings and incorporating a number of ideals. While it would be foolish to claim that design is improving the lives of the majority of the British public, it does seem to be expanding its sphere of influence.

The naivety of the ideals expressed in 1946 was both its strength and its weakness. What must be tackled now is a re-assertion of those aims, this time presented within a more sophisticated understanding of the structures upon which they depend. 1986 might well be the year to repeat the claim that Britain *Can* Make It.

FURTHER READING

Architectural Review, 'Industrial design – special issue', vol 100 no 598, October 1946.

Austen, Peter 'Britain Can Make It: the Council of Industrial Design', *Graphis*, vol 2 no 14, March-April 1946.

Black, Misha (ed) *Exhibition Design*, Architectural Press, London, 1950.

Black, Misha 'Dissecting the problem and Exhibition Design', *Art and Industry*, September 1948.

Board of Trade Journal, 'Britain Can Make It. The exhibition of post-war products', 28 September 1946, supplement.

Carrington, Noel *Industrial Design in Britain*, Pilot Press, 1947.

Carrington, Noel 'Britain Can Make It', *Journal of the Royal Society of Arts*, 27 September 1946.

Council of Industrial Design, *First Annual Report 1945–46*, 1946.

Council of Industrial Design, *Britain Can Make It*, exhibition catalogue, HMSO, 1946.

Council of Industrial Design, *Design '46. Survey of British industrial design as displayed at the 'Britain Can Make It' exhibition*, edited by W H Newman, 1946.

Council of Industrial Design *Design Quiz*, HMSO, 1946.

Council of Industrial Design *Furnishing to fit the family*, HMSO, 1947.

Council of Industrial Design *Four Ways of Living*, introduced by Frank Mansfield, HMSO, 1949.

Department of Overseas Trade, *Report of the committee under the chairmanship of Lord Ramsden to consider the part which exhibitions and fairs should play in the promotion of export trade in the post-war era to advise on the policy and plans to be adopted to drive the maximum advantage from such displays*, HMSO, 1946.

Floud, Peter 'British exhibitions of selected designs', *Design*, no 87, March 1956.

Form (Sweden) 'Britain Can Make It', no 9, 1946.

Gardner, James and Heller, Caroline *Exhibition and Display*, Batsford, London, 1960.

Gaunt, William, 'Design makes good', *Evening Standard*, 25 September 1946.

Gray, Milner *The Practice of Design*, 1946.

S C Leslie 'Britain Can Make It — overseas buyers' interest in exhibition', *The Times*, 1946.

Luckhurst, K W *The Story of Exhibitions*, Studio, London, 1951.

Mortimer, Raymond 'Britain Can Make It!', *New Statesman and Nation*, 28 September 1946.

Pick, Beverley 'Displaying the Ideal Home', *Art and Industry*, July 1948.

Sissons, Michael & French, Philip (eds) *The Age of Austerity*, Hodder & Stoughton, London, 1963.

The Studio Yearbook: Decorative Art 1943–48, 1948.

Sunday Times 'Britain Can Make It — some criticisms', 29 September 1946.

Weiner, Martin *English Culture and the Decline of the Industrial Spirit*, Cambridge University Press, 1984.

Woodham, Jonathan *The Industrial Designer and the Public*, Pembridge Press, History of Design series, 1983.

3 575 8